CW00688815

'This book questions our relationship with kn
understanding of intelligence and considers wh
the age of machines. Rose Luckin's belief that
be the crucial agents of change in our approacı   ... . a
vitally important read for anyone interested in preparing a generation of
young people for what lies ahead.'

**Lord Puttnam, Member of the House of Lords Select Committee
on Artificial Intelligence**

'This is a fascinating examination of intelligence. Rose Luckin successfully
unpacks the relationship between intelligence, knowledge and information,
and clarifies the competitive advantage of the elements of human
intelligence over artificial intelligence. Her case for urgently moving to an
intelligence-based curriculum is compelling.'

**Lord Jim Knight, Chief Education and External Officer, Tes,
and former Schools Minister**

'This highly accessible book offers a thoughtful, personal exploration
of what it means to know. From this critical foundation Luckin offers a
many-faceted consideration of intelligence as it applies to humans and as
it might apply to non-human systems. Her observations on what all this
means for education make this a book anyone concerned with the policy
and practice of teaching and learning should read.'

Angela McFarlane, Trustee, Education Development Trust

'Few people, if any, understand the future of machine learning and AI, and
their applications to education, better than Rose Luckin. There is no more
important topic for those involved in education to comprehend. There is
no better guide than this book.'

Sir Anthony Seldon, Vice-Chancellor, University of Buckingham

Machine Learning and Human Intelligence

Machine Learning and Human Intelligence

The future of education for the 21st century

Rosemary Luckin

IOE Press

First published in 2018 by the UCL Institute of Education Press, University College London, 20 Bedford Way, London WC1H 0AL

www.ucl-ioe-press.com

© Rosemary Luckin 2018

British Library Cataloguing in Publication Data:
A catalogue record for this publication is available from the British Library

ISBNs
978-1-78277-251-4 (paperback)
978-1-78277-257-6 (PDF eBook)
978-1-78277-258-3 (ePub eBook)
978-1-78277-259-0 (Kindle eBook)

All rights reserved. No part of this publication may be reproduced, stored in a retrieval system or transmitted in any form or by any means, electronic, mechanical, photocopying, recording or otherwise, without the prior permission of the copyright owner.

Every effort has been made to trace copyright holders and to obtain their permission for the use of copyright material. The publisher apologizes for any errors or omissions and would be grateful if notified of any corrections that should be incorporated in future reprints or editions of this book.

The opinions expressed in this publication are those of the authors and do not necessarily reflect the views of the UCL Institute of Education, University College London.

Typeset by Quadrant Infotech (India) Pvt Ltd
Printed by CPI Group (UK) Ltd, Croydon, CR0 4YY
Cover image © Ariel Skelley/DigitalVision/Getty Images

Contents

Acknowledgements

Completing this book would have been a long and lonely journey without the help and support of numerous people. I have been lucky and privileged to have benefited from the most interested and supportive colleagues, and I would like to give special thanks to Dr Mutlu Cukurova and all the members of the UCL Knowledge Lab, Sir Anthony Seldon, Lord Jim Knight, Prof. Judy Kay, Priya Lakhani and the inspirational OPPI community, to name but a few. Thank you for your constructive criticism, encouragement and general feedback on the work and thinking at the heart of this enterprise. Many thanks also to the educators and learners with whom I have been lucky enough to work over the past few years and to the amazing team at the UCL IOE Press, especially Pat Gordon-Smith. My friends have been a constant source of support and inspiration – particular thanks to Paul, Kim and Phil for the great conversations and thought provocation. Lastly, words are inadequate to express my thanks for the constant support of my family who always encourage and inform my work, in particular my appreciation to Catherine, who read and commented on every word of this text. I dedicate this book to my grandchildren, Dexter and Imogen: may your striving to extend your human intelligence be supremely enjoyable.

Chapter 1

Intelligence, human and artificial

On 10 June 1983 my first child was born: a son whom we named James. To this day I remember gazing with wonder at this tiny person snuggling down beside me. The emotions I felt in that moment were so potent that I believed they might burst out of me. He smelt amazing, his skin was so soft and his breath so gentle. Anyone who is a parent will understand the wave of all-consuming love that one feels for a child in those moments after birth and indeed for the rest of one's life. Along with the love and joy and excitement I experienced on that day, I also felt an overwhelming sense of responsibility; here was a tiny, perfectly formed person, not yet able to look after himself and completely dependent on me for his future well-being. I was charged with making sure that he was safe and happy, and that he fulfilled all of his potential as a member of society.

The birth and subsequent development of a child is my number one wonder of the world. It is unparalleled by any of the amazing features of the physical world manifested in waterfalls, mountains, lakes or seas. The pure beauty of a soprano's song, the taste of an exquisite meal, the smell of freshly baked bread, ground coffee or orange blossom on a warm summer's day: these wonders are merely a drop in the ocean of complexity that pervades this world and the surrounding cosmos. And yet, we believe that we can capture the human capacities that enable us to appreciate this mass of complexity and wonder and experience, explain and communicate it to others. We believe that we can somehow measure this complex intelligence through some form of standardized metric.

In our current time, we are obsessed with measuring things about ourselves in order to gain comfort that everything is normal, or to measure ourselves against each other to illustrate who is doing best and who is not performing or behaving as well as they should be. I know that in those first few days after my son's birth I was told what percentile he fell in for his weight, his length and the size of his head. When I took him to the baby clinic he was weighed on a regular basis and his weight was compared to that which was considered normal for a baby of his age. There are good reasons why we take these measurements: we want to ensure that babies are well fed and well looked after. But, I suggest that our obsession with measurement has got the better of us when it comes to trying to quantify every aspect of our being and, in particular, our intelligence.

We too easily defer to authority to tell us how we should measure things, what we should accept as evidence of why we can know something or believe it to be true. We no longer trust our eyes and noses when it comes to deciding if food is fresh: we need a label and a sell by date. We need a continuous battery of standardized tests to decide whether our children are learning and we judge people's popularity, or dare I say their worth, by the number of Facebook friends they can muster.

As a scientist, I love evidence, but I also value judgement and the ability to make decisions about the validity of that evidence. However, I fear that, in general, we humans have fallen into the trap of needing an authority to tell us how to value things: that authority might be the Food Standards Authority or a retailer; it might be a qualifications provider, or it might even be a large technology company. We defer too easily to this authority rather than using our intelligence to make up our own minds about how we should value things, what we should believe and what we can know. I fear that we have also been suckered into choosing that authority without much question. We may perhaps choose them because others value them, because someone we respect has told us that they are an authority, or because history or tradition has put them in the position of being an authority. Perhaps we trust them because they are familiar, or because their metrics are understandable. I suggest, however, that we too rarely think about why we regard someone or something as an authority. I am not saying that we need to question every figure of authority, but I am suggesting that we need to know why we trust an authority and when that trust needs to be tested through seeking out good solid evidence and data to help us judge who and what we believe. I am concerned that our obsession with measuring and simplicity is robbing us of our ability to think and decide for ourselves what is of value. Worse still it is causing us to value things inappropriately. In particular, it is leading us to oversimplify and undervalue human intelligence, and to value artificial intelligence inappropriately.

One has only to look at the global financial crisis of 2008 to see our inability to recognize real authority and make good evidence-based judgements in action. People were persuaded into investing in bonds that were backed by subprime mortgages. Mortgagees were inevitably going to default on these mortgages when their initially low interest rates were increased. Large, allegedly knowledgeable investors bought into these worthless securities because they trusted the authority of the banks who were creating and selling the bonds. Even when a few people started to probe the underlying mortgage components in these bonds and to raise concerns, they were ignored – because they were not the recognized authority and were suggesting something was happening that had never happened before. Their views were uncomfortable. I suggest that this is evidence that people had lost, or at least were closing their senses to, their ability to make wise judgements about the validity of evidence (Lewis, 2011). We risk a similar problem today with instances of 'fake news' gaining far too much credibility.

What is intelligence and why does it matter?

For the purposes of this book, I am going to narrow down the area of human enterprise that we need to value effectively. I am going to focus on the way that we try to make decisions about people's abilities, their intellectual capacity, their *intelligence*. We do this from a young age and we continue to do it throughout our lives. We don't limit ourselves to comparing individual people against each other; we also compare country to country to see whose students are performing the best in their schools, colleges and universities, for example through the OECD PISA assessments (OECD, 2018). I will focus on intelligence, because intelligence is at the heart of what makes us human.

In particular, I will explore the way in which we make decisions about whether or not somebody or something is intelligent, and how we constantly try and quantify this intelligence into a reassuringly large number. I will examine the implications for our education systems of the way that we perceive intelligence, talk about intelligence and evaluate intelligence. This examination will be conducted within the context of a world that is increasingly augmented by *artificial* intelligence (AI). Writing this book is a pragmatic enterprise in which I unpack the elements of *human* intelligence that we need to value. I use what I unpack to make one central argument, and then consider what our response should be. I argue that the methods we use for identifying, talking about and valuing human intelligence are impoverished. As a consequence of these impoverished tools we are dumbing down, not smarting up, the most valuable resource in the world: ourselves.

Worse still, our impoverished evaluation of human intelligence is leading us to overvalue the intelligence manifested in the latest technology – to put at risk the future of humanity because we are not judging wisely the evidence of what is happening around us in our world. I say this as someone who has studied and developed artificial intelligence systems for use in education for over 25 years. Indeed, I champion the use of well-designed AI in education, and believe that AI can be invaluable to assist human learning and teaching. It is precisely this intimate relationship with AI that leads me to question how we perceive AI.

But before I go any further, I need to define what I mean by *intelligence*. According to the *Oxford English Dictionary*, intelligence is the 'faculty of understanding, or intellect'. As a noun, intelligence is a mental 'capacity to understand'. If we look up *understanding*, its definition as a noun is 'knowledge', and as a verb it is the ability 'to comprehend; to apprehend the meaning or import of' or 'to grasp the idea of' something. If we *know* something we are 'acquainted with' it and have a 'familiarity gained by experience'.

Intuitively, this makes sense. However, these definitions give us no indication about how we might evaluate the intelligence of a person, or anything else.

In reality, definitions like this make intelligence sound like something we either have or don't have at any particular moment in time. Definitions are often not the best tool to use when one is trying to understand a complex concept such as intelligence. It is clear that human intelligence is aligned with intellect, with complex cognitive processes, with the understanding of the knowledge, skills and abilities both of others and of ourselves. It is our intelligence that enables us to learn, to apply our knowledge, to synthesize what we know in order to solve problems, to communicate with others, to make decisions, to think, to express and to learn from experience. It is certainly about a great deal more than what we learn in school.

Over the decades we have changed our conceptions of what it means to be intelligent and how we evaluate our intelligence. For example, the Socratic Paradox dates back to Plato (Wikipedia, n.d.b.) and is embodied in the phrase 'he knew he was intelligent because he knew that he knew nothing'. Einstein is believed to have equated intelligence with imagination (Quora, 2016) and the admissions tutors in the early days of Harvard University saw intelligence in a person's ability to speak a variety of languages, including Latin, Hebrew and Greek (*New York Times*, n.d.). More recently, as we have moved towards wanting to quantify and measure intelligence, we have formulated tests that people can take to provide a score that can be used to evaluate their intelligence.

At the start of the 20th century the intelligence test was introduced with the Simon-Binet test, which was formulated when French psychologists were asked to determine which children might need additional help at school. The concept of an intelligence quotient or IQ was born. Each person was deemed to have a particular IQ that was calculated by dividing by that person's chronological age the total score he or she achieved across several standardized tests that had been specifically designed to assess human intelligence. Proponents of these tests happily admit that the scores are only estimates of a person's intelligence, because the concept of intelligence is itself abstract. Over the years IQ scores have been used to determine what educational system is best for a particular individual, and to evaluate their suitability for a job or their entitlement to be described as having a particular disability.

New forms of testing have been developed: the Wechsler Scales (1939), for example, include non-verbal items; the Bayley Scales of Infant Development (1969) are used for children under age two; and the British Ability Scales (1979). The meaning and measurement of intelligence remain open to question, and interest in their study has been renewed by the advent of AI applied at scale. The nature of the connection between intelligence and education is also increasingly challenged (Roth *et al.*, 2015), with discussions energized once again by the increasing role of AI in the workplace and the accompanying demands for changes to education, training and assessment (Luckin, 2017a).

In chapters 2 and 3, I will go into some detail about the 'nuts and bolts' of intelligence, which will include exploring the core concepts of knowledge, understanding and familiarity gained through experience, as expressed in the *Oxford English Dictionary* definitions of intelligence described earlier. In the rest of this chapter I want to whet your appetite for the story ahead by introducing some of the key ingredients in the argument of this book: the social basis of intelligence and the importance of human development, the role of human instinct and luck, and the value of good evidence.

Human development and the social basis of thought and intelligence

An IQ score is a snapshot in time, but intelligence is not static – it is something that develops over time. It is the development of intelligence that enabled the tiny baby born on that day in 1983 to become the mature adult who now has responsibility for children of his own. The relationship between an intelligence test result and the extent to which an individual has developed over time is poorly represented by the IQ test score, which merely divides the total score from a set of intelligence tests by their chronological age. Chronological age is not a precise determinant of developmental stage. If it were then all children would develop at exactly the same rate, but we know that there are many individual differences between children that mean chronological age is not always a good determinant of developmental stage.

I find it hard to equate the complexity of human intellect with the insufficiency of an IQ test. I acknowledge that there is abundant evidence that demonstrates the correlation between IQ test scores and mortality, between IQ test scores and school achievement, and between IQ test scores and verbal fluency (see, for example, Gottfredson and Deary, 2016; American Psychological Association, 1996; Jackson, 2002). However, the IQ test for me is still grossly inadequate, both in and of itself as a static measure of intelligence at any moment in time and as a way of recognizing something that has a strong developmental characteristic. Intelligence is something that we can continue to develop throughout our lives provided we escape the clutches of dementia or other psychological disability. We therefore need to think about intelligence in this continually developing way. Intelligence is never a finished product; intelligence is constantly evolving and developing.

A dissatisfaction with the adequacy of IQ tests was one of the factors that motivated the Russian psychologist Lev Vygotsky to search for an alternative way of describing the developing intellect of humans, particularly young humans of school age. Vygotsky believed that children's development was the result of their interactions with other people. These interactions experienced by children as they develop are the building blocks for the psychological processes that build the intellect of that child.

The strength of Vygotsky's statement, often referred to as the law of cultural development, is that it implies that each person's intellectual capacity is a product of the society within which they live. This in turn means that society bears a huge responsibility for the intellectual development of its members. The societies that create the richest opportunities for social interaction that expand the intellectual capacities of their members will be the societies that have the greatest communal intellectual power. This law of cultural development permits an interpretation of the surge of responsibility I felt at the birth of my son, which confirms that my feelings of responsibility were entirely appropriate.

The work of Vygotsky (1978; 1986; 1987), or perhaps more accurately the translations of the work of Vygotsky from his native Russian, have come under considerable criticism in recent years (for example, Yasnitsky and van der Veer, 2015). These criticisms are mainly based upon the poor quality of the translations of Vygotsky's work to English, wherein there are discrepancies and errors. Nevertheless, I find much value in the work that has been published in English. For example, I am attracted by Vygotsky's evaluation of human activity as being much more than the external performance celebrated by the behaviourist thinkers prevalent at the time of his work, such as Thorndike (1911; 1914), Watson (1926) and Skinner (1991; 1957). I am also persuaded by the work of other respected writers, such as Jerome Bruner (1996), who recognized the importance of the emphasis that Vygotsky placed upon the role of societal consciousness in individual human cognition. He suggests that this is the revolutionary aspect of Vygotsky's work, and proposes that the role of societal consciousness should be seen as the coalescence of collectivism and consciousness. In addition, I trust the evidence of my own scientific research over the past decades and make my judgements about the validity of Vygotsky's work, based upon a variety of evidence, while at the same time acknowledging that what I have read, and what I describe here as being the words of Vygotsky, may more accurately be described as the words of the translators of his work, inspired by what he actually wrote. In other words, I read Vygotsky with my intellectual eyes open.

Vygotsky's work on human intellect and consciousness introduced a developmental approach in which elementary psychological processes, such as involuntary memory, form the foundation of human behaviour and are the result of evolutionary development. They are shared by animals and humans alike. The higher psychological processes, such as creative imagination and rational thinking, are specific to humans and cannot be explained in the same fashion as the elementary, involuntary processes. The key difference can be found in the social, interpersonal activity that is essential to human thinking. I'll refer to these higher psychological processes as advanced human thinking. It is this advanced human thinking that is the foundation of our human intelligence.

Advanced human thinking processes evolved from and through our ability to communicate with each other and work together cooperatively. In the same way that we use physical tools to achieve tasks, such as baking a cake, building a wall or writing a book, we use the tools of gesture and spoken or written language to communicate with each other and organize our communal and cooperative working. It was the development of these communicative sign systems, such as language, that enabled humans to think beyond our physical interactions in the world. We can think and talk about things of which we have no direct physical experience. We are capable of abstract thought.

Sign systems, such as language, mediate the way that we respond to the stimuli we receive about the physical and social world around us. These mediating sign systems are the building blocks of our advanced human thinking processing. The emergence of speech was as important to Vygotsky as the emergence of socially organized labour was to Marx and Engels. As expressed in the law of cultural development, any search for the sources of human intelligence must focus on the social history of an individual's interactions, rather than on their individual psychological processes, their biological maturation or their genetic inheritance alone. If we are to look at our social interactions to identify and evaluate our advanced human thinking and our intelligence, then IQ tests miss the mark. I am not suggesting that IQ tests are totally useless, I am saying that they only tell us a small part of the story about intelligence. They tell us about our individual advanced human thinking with respect to the particular sort of thinking that needs to be applied to the completion of the IQ tests.

I will set aside the notion of communal intelligence for now but will return to it in Chapter 4. Now I want to address the problem of how the processes that happen between people become the thoughts of the human mind. The link between our social activity and the psychological processes of our mind is referred to by Vygotsky as internalization. Internalization is a complex process through which each of us gains control over the signs, such as language, that we use for our social activity. As we gain control over these *external* signs they are transformed into the signs *of our thinking*, a process that can be described as the semiosis of the mind. The process of internalization means that the way that we interact together in culturally different ways results in culturally different ways of processing our thoughts. The languages that we use for our various social interactions, and that therefore influence the internal language that we use for our thinking, also enable us to organize ourselves and to pass on our thoughts and languages to inform future generations. There is no history without the language of social interaction.

In my earlier discussions about IQ tests and scores, I stressed that I wanted a developmental aspect to any specification of intelligence. A Vygotskian lens provides us with a process through which an individual's mental functioning develops as an interaction between that individual and their sociocultural environment. The nature of the social environment influences the nature of a person's resultant mental processes. The crystallization of this process of internalization can be found in the theoretical construct for which Vygotsky is probably best known: the zone of proximal development, or ZPD. The ZPD was introduced for the context of school-aged children, because school-aged children were considered to be particularly sensitive to the benefits of instruction and the ZPD is crucially about instruction. It is, however, useful to note that the processes considered to be integral to the ZPD have been observed subsequently by researchers with much younger children (Rogoff *et al.*, 1984; Valsiner, 1984) and with adults (for example Shabani, 2016). The ZPD describes the most fertile interactions which occur between members of a culture, for example as part of an educational institution and as a learner. These are the interactions that will have the greatest impact upon that individual learner's development and intelligence. I will return to this discussion in Chapter 6 when I consider how education can better prepare people for their intelligent future.

Here, I want to concentrate on the social basis of thought, consciousness and intelligence and the reason why I am attracted to Vygotsky's work so much. I believe that intelligence is fundamentally connected to one's ability to interact socially. Intelligence is not only born out of social interaction; it is increasingly manifested in social interaction. When I say intelligence here, I am referring to the full-blown rich concept of human intelligence, not the mastery of a particular tranche of knowledge or the skill that enables us to get a high score on an IQ test. I will expand upon what I mean by the full-blown rich concept of human intelligence in Chapter 2, but I am flagging up now that social interaction is fundamental to a modern conception of intelligence. It is the type of intelligent that we need to be as we progress through the 21st century, an intelligence that is human, that emanates from our emotional, sensory and self-effective understanding of ourselves and of our peers. This type of intelligence is at the heart of humanity and is vital for our future well-being.

The role of human instinct and luck in our intelligence

Human instinct is often thought of as behaviours that appear to be innate and rational but that are actually performed without conscious intention. These innate behaviours are not the result of some learning process: to use the language of Vygotsky, they are not mediated. They are the behavioural responses of a living organism to a stimulus. However, they are also not completely disconnected from the complex behaviours of the advanced human thinking processes that we associate with intelligence. There is a connection between our instinct and our intelligence.

To help me develop and explain the connection between our instincts and our intelligence, I am going to use a way of talking about the human mind that has become very popular in recent years, largely thanks to the work of Nobel prize-winning economic scientist Daniel Kahneman from Princeton University. Kahneman expands on previous work completed by psychologists like Keith Stanovich (2009a; 2009b; 2016), who introduced the idea that the human mind has two systems. System 1 is automatic and is outside our voluntary control. This is the system that we might consider to be the home of our instincts. System 2 is the effortful system that is the home of strenuous mental effort. It is the mind of complex thinking, and of human agency; it is within our voluntary control. It is this System 2 mind that we generally associate with intelligence. The suggestion here is not that our minds are literally split into two systems, but rather that it is useful to think in terms of our thinking being part of two connected but different systems.

The important point from my perspective is that System 2 intellect depends on System 1 instinct. In other words, the intelligent mind that we cherish so much cannot exist without our instinctive System 1 mind (Kahneman, 2011; Kahneman and Tversky, 2000). System 1 is the home of our ability to perceive the world around us and to recognize objects, to shy away from hot, cold and pain and to detect when the person we are talking to is angry. However, System 1 is more than a set of innate responses to stimuli; it is also the mind of learned associations that can be increased and speeded up through practice. It includes abilities and skills such as reading simple text and riding a bicycle. The behaviours that result from the mental processing of System 1 require little or no effort and appear to occur automatically. However, in many cases, they are the result of much practice.

Humans do not all share the same abilities and skills within System 1, because some of our System 1 results from specialist practice, such as advanced driving skills or the ability to determine intuitively that a particular chess move is a good one. The actions that result from our System 1 processing include involuntary ones, and others that we *could* control, but that *we do not generally control*. Every car driver has experienced that moment when they arrive at their destination only to realize that they don't fully remember their journey. They feel as if they were on 'autopilot'. This is the skilled practice that now resides in our System 1 mind.

The differentiating factor of System 2 thinking is that it requires our conscious attention. From the parallel parking dreaded by all learner drivers, to the attention that I award to the process of writing this book, all of our System 2 behaviours stop when we allow our attention to be distracted elsewhere. We can also use our System 2 mind to exert control over our System 1 mind. For example, by intervening in our normally automatic functioning, in order to focus our thinking on a particular activity: planning a complex route against a tight deadline, learning a tricky element of calculus or studying the nuances in the relationship between Shakespeare's King Lear and his three daughters.

These times when we deliberately exert our control to bring our attention to a particular activity are the times when we are focusing our attention effectively on just one activity, and it is perfectly possible that we can miss what is happening around us. The man with the trolley bag who is about to hit us as we look at the train station's departures board, the car crash that happens outside the window of the school where we are studying calculus or the fact that it has started raining during a performance of *King Lear* at the Globe Theatre in London. Even when these extraneous activities are pointed out to us, we sometimes don't believe that we missed them: the man with the trolley bag came out of nowhere, as did the car that crashed outside the window; as for the rain, what rain? As Daniel Kahneman elegantly tells us 'we can be blind to the obvious and we are also blind to our blindness' (Kahneman, 2011: 26).

The relevance of System 1 and System 2 thinking for my purpose here can be found in the relationship that exists between these two systems of the mind. System 1 is like the energetic toddler constantly demanding that System 2 react to its actions. System 2 is something of a laid-back parent most of the time, because most of the time everything is progressing normally. System 2 therefore usually accepts what System 1 is suggesting, and System 2 beliefs and actions are formulated as a result. We only become conscious of System 1 when we need System 2 to act in a more concerted manner, because we are faced with a situation that requires greater processing and action – action beyond the already learnt and partially automated processes and skills that have become part of System 1.

System 2 is also in control of what we know about ourselves, of the way that we regulate our thinking, of the all-important metacognitive knowledge and skills that help us to develop our self-efficacy. Self-efficacy is vital to our human intelligence and something that I will discuss in more detail throughout this book.

The relationship between our System 1 and System 2 minds is not all plain sailing. There are some problems that arise with our energetic System 1 through its automatic and often unavoidable actions. These automatic actions mean that we behave in biased ways, without even realizing. For example, over the years I have realized that I am overly sympathetic to a particular type of person. These people are always positive and animated, full of interesting things to say, having experienced a rich and varied life. When such people suggest to me that I should do something that seems out of line with what I believe to be appropriate, I will always give them the benefit of the doubt. I will require far less evidence to follow their advice than I will require from a quieter, less effusive individual. I know that I have this bias and yet I still get sucked in by these people. I am getting better at recognizing the situation and reigning in my desire to follow the lead of my lively friends. However, this reigning-in of my bias is difficult: it takes a lot of effort and I don't always succeed.

In the example of my unhelpful bias towards a particular type of person, I could wish that my System 2 had more get up and go and did more to control energetic System 1. In emergencies, however, such as when I see that the man with the trolley bag who is about to hit me on the station while I am studying the departure board has a cup of hot coffee in his hand, I am only too pleased that System 1 has taken control, made me move, and reduced the likelihood of my coming to harm.

I want to make one final point before we move on. This point relates to work done more recently by the originators of the System 1, System 2 theory: Stanovich and West (2008). Their work was focused on trying to explain why some people were more susceptible to bias. Their proposal is that our System 2 actually consists of two separate subsystems. Subsystem 1 is the system of complex computation, of slow deliberate thinking and the completion of IQ tests: it is called the algorithmic subsystem. This subsystem is able to switch from one task to another and behave extremely efficiently. People who have a particularly highly developed subsystem 1 within their System 2 mind score highly when it comes IQ evaluations.

However, this is not the whole story. There is a second subsystem within our System 2 minds. This is the subsystem that allows us to ignore our biases, to keep that energetic, attention-needing toddler of our System 1 under control. It means that we are not tempted into accepting an intuitively attractive proposition without engaging our System 2 minds in some strenuous mental effort. This second subsystem is the one that keeps us paying attention: it maintains our focus and our self-control, even when we are tired. This is what helps us to combat the natural laziness of our System 2 mind. Stanovich has called this second subsystem the 'rational subsystem' of our System 2 minds. People with a stronger rational subsystem have been shown to be more able to cope with cognitive load, and to avoid ego depletion. Ego depletion is what happens when our self-control becomes less effective because all our voluntary efforts have diminished our overall mental energy. There is evidence that the power of people's rational subsystem is a better predictor of their ability than the traditional intelligence tests that measure the powers of the algorithmic subsystem only.

'Rationality' feels like far too mundane a label for this vital second subsystem within our System 2 mind. It deserves a more sophisticated sounding appellation that encompasses the imagination so cherished by

Einstein and the ingredients of our knowing self. It needs a word to convey that this subsystem means we can act upon our realization of what we do and do not know in a manner that is accurately goal-directed and effective; that we are able to act based on an appropriate interpretation of the suggestions and emotions that our overactive System 1 is constantly pushing in front of us. It needs a word that means we can regulate our responses too. I suggest that 'self-efficacy' might be such a word.

I will talk more about intelligence in chapters 2 and 3, and I will link this 'rational' subsystem with the concept of self-efficacy. In my consideration of self-efficacy, I will explore the concept of self-efficacy as an amalgam of metacognitive knowledge, skill and regulation that combine with appropriately directed motivation. In this scenario, the algorithmic *sub*system of our effortful mind delivers the accurate, evidence-based metacognitive knowledge and skills. The rational *sub*system of our effortful mind provides the metacognitive regulation and goal-directed motivation. Both of these subsystems are fundamental to human intelligence, but we currently overvalue the algorithmic mind to the detriment of the rational. I will also consider further the importance of System 1's automatic thinking, and our sensory experience of the world, to which we also give too little credence when it comes to consideration of what makes us intelligent.

Ah, but what of luck, I hear you ask? I said I would discuss instinct *and* luck. Luck is like cayenne pepper is to cheese in a classic sauce, or like a pinch of sugar is to tomatoes in a favourite pasta sauce: it makes all the difference to our experiences of the world. We do not like to acknowledge the role that luck plays in our lives because it is not within our full control. There are people who say that you can 'make your own luck', but as I look at the starving children in the poorest parts of the world who will not benefit from the wonders that a good education can provide, it is obvious that they are not lucky, and that they are not able to change this situation.

However, we desire to see ourselves as rational, intelligent humans, who are in control of much of our destiny. We do not like to think that luck has such a significant role in our success. We are therefore prone to post hoc rationalization about what has happened to us and about what has happened to other people, so that we can explain things without the need to acknowledge any legitimate role for luck.

Early in my academic career, I learnt something about the power of a good story. My first job as a research fellow following on from my PhD was on a project that was exploring the role narrative plays in how we construct our understanding of the world in order to learn and to acquire knowledge. It is that same power of narrative that leads us to massively inaccurate post hoc rationalizations about the power of our human capacity. We tell ourselves stories that explain why something has happened, why someone is successful, why we have done well in an examination or won a game of bridge. We do this because attributing any part of these success stories to luck would undermine the way that we evaluate ourselves as sentient, intelligent people. And yet Lady Luck provides the X-factor that makes all the difference. We need to find a way to acknowledge the role that luck plays in our conceptualization of intelligence.

The value of good evidence

The final key feature of intelligence that I want to discuss is the nature of evidence and what makes evidence sound, and therefore what makes it the sort of thing that we should take notice of as we adjust our actions and behaviours. The evidence that I shall discuss here is the evidence that we observe and experience in the wider world. It is the evidence of our own knowledge and understanding that enables us to act with self-efficacy, as intelligent people. It is an important feature of our intelligence.

My work as a research scientist requires a good eye for solid evidence. It demands the skill to design appropriate methods to collect data, the expertise to analyse that data and the capacity to extract from that analysis the key findings and conclusions. It also demands that I am able to synthesize the findings from multiple data sources and analyse them to extract the conclusions that will drive my future research. I must also be able to make judgements about the quality of the evidence reported from the research conducted by my peers and colleagues and as reported in the papers and books that they publish.

I am particularly interested in evidence that tells us something about whether and how technology, especially technology that uses artificial intelligence, does or does not help learners to learn and/or teachers to teach. People like me who are involved in developing educational applications for technologies have been told time and time again that we need to demonstrate 'that the technology works'. I therefore spend a lot of time and effort unpacking what we mean when we say technology that 'works' and describing what we actually want it to do. I also work with other educational developers, particularly entrepreneurs who have founded or who work for small companies, to help them understand how they might best evidence whether and how their 'technology works'.

Over the years I have developed a good nose for what constitutes solid evidence: I would be lost without this. I have also come to realize that this finely tuned 'nose' is the result of years of practice and learning. I confronted this realization in no uncertain terms recently when my colleague Dr Mutlu Cukurova and I were developing a training course to help the entrepreneurs we work with to understand research evidence. We wanted them to know how to interpret findings reported from research studies, and to know how to design their own data collection and analysis to help them understand whether their products or services were doing what they had intended for the learners and teachers for whom they design. I have to say at this point that Mutlu, a very talented academic, was doing all the hard work. He designed an excellent training course.

When the first cohort of entrepreneurs enthusiastically commenced our research training we soon realized that the course was far too complex for people who were highly intelligent but preoccupied with running a business. We needed to extract the important essence of the course and, as Einstein is reputed to have said, make it as simple as it could be, but no simpler. Mutlu rewrote the entire course.

The second cohort of entrepreneurs benefited from this much-improved offering. They enjoyed its challenge and learnt from its wisdom. This experience has confirmed my view that many people could benefit greatly from help in understanding what evidence really is, how to make their own judgements about what they believe, and how they are going to act as a result of those beliefs. The concern that we do not train people to recognize good evidence, so they can make appropriate decisions about what is fake and what is reality, has been exemplified in the rush of stories about the way that social media is manipulating people's views and opinions. I read frequently about the echo chamber of Twitter, and the proliferation of phoney press and faux expertise. If we do not educate people to differentiate effectively between what is true, what is false and what is just opinion about which they need to draw their own conclusions from evidence, then it is not surprising that people are easily duped by the ersatz fodder of the internet. I am *not* suggesting that everyone should do a comprehensive literature review every time they see a news story on twitter. But I *am* suggesting that we can all develop the skill and knowledge to approach those news stories with a critical eye, and an idea about where and how we might seek evidence when we want to.

In Chapter 2, I write about how easily we confuse information and knowledge. Information is the data that needs to be analysed and synthesized in order to extract the features from which we construct our knowledge and understanding. Here, I want to attend to the importance of the questions that we ask, because it is these questions that will drive the decisions we make about what is and what it is not solid evidence.

Mutlu and I homed in on the idea that the most important thing we needed to do to help our entrepreneurs understand research evidence was to teach them how to ask the right question. Knowing how to ask the right question is relevant to understanding existing research publications and reports, and to knowing what data to collect and analyse to understand if and how a technology 'works'. As a research academic, I know that before I even start to think about which data I might need to collect, or which evidence I might want to collate from existing research, I must spend considerable time deciding what question I want to ask from this evidence. We should not therefore have been surprised to discover that we needed to help our entrepreneurs to appreciate the importance of this first step. In these days of big data, it is very easy to forget the importance of working out what you want to ask of all the data at your fingertips.

To help our entrepreneurs ask the right research questions to drive their study design, we help them to differentiate between a good idea and a research question. We try to open their minds by questioning the nature of the problem situation that their technology is intended to address. We point out that there are different sorts of questions that can be asked about the same problem situation. For example, I may want to find out more about the problem that I believe exists, in which case I will ask exploratory questions. Alternatively, I might want to try to work out what can be done to address this problem and consider whether my proposed intervention is likely to work. Or I might want to actually change the situation and see if that addresses the problem. We encourage our entrepreneurs to probe why a question is right for their business, why it is relevant to their customers, whether or not it permits rigorous management of the potential biases and subjectivities that may occur. We get them to make sure that they are not making assumptions of which they are not aware, and we also draw their attention to the language they use in their research question. They need to make sure that their terminology is well defined and clearly articulated.

A second tool that we use to help our entrepreneurs in their studies is a theory of change: a comprehensive description of how and why a desired change is expected to happen in a particular context (Center for Theory of Change, 2017). We introduce them to the concept of a theory of change logic model (W.K. Kellogg Foundation, 2006) to describe their business's intervention and activities. Through the logic model the intervention is linked to the outcomes and impact that they hope their technology will produce. The aim of engaging our entrepreneurs in the creation of these logic models is to help them connect the activities they are doing with the outcomes they desire. The entrepreneurs often struggle to identify the measurable primary impact they are intending their product or service to achieve, and the activities associated with this impact.

This logic modelling process sets the scene for our entrepreneurs to tackle the really hard task of designing the question that they want their research study to address. At this stage, we also tackle the thorny subject of our beliefs about the nature and scope of knowledge and how we come to know about the world: this is commonly referred to as epistemology. There are many books about epistemology, written by scholars who are far better able to explain this complex concept then I am (see, for example, Hofer and Pintrich, 2002). However, I will endeavour to introduce the key elements of epistemology in order to convince you that we must and can include it in our conceptualizations of human intelligence. We complete a similar task with our entrepreneurs because it is important for them to know that the methodology they choose to gather the evidence about how and if their technology 'works' will be driven by their underlying epistemological assumptions.

Epistemology is extremely important to what we believe knowledge is and how we believe we come to know something. The subject of personal knowledge is discussed in many parts of this book, and in Chapter 2 we consider the notion of our personal epistemology and how it impacts upon the way we learn. For the purposes of the discussion here, I will consider epistemology in its more general sense as concerning our beliefs about the nature and scope of knowledge and how we come to know about the world. It is important for our entrepreneurs to know that the methodology they choose will be driven by their epistemological assumptions.

When it comes to discussions about how we know something about the world, there are two extreme positions, and various stances in between. The first extreme is the positivist one. The positivist believes that there is a reality in the world that will provide one true explanation if only we can find it. This position is remarkably resilient and many of our entrepreneurs start from this belief. Their initial attraction is often to experimental research designs, often involving randomised controlled trials (RCT) and quantitative data analysis. They believe that this approach will enable them to 'prove' that their particular technology product or service has a positive, statistically significant impact on its users. Our goal is to open their eyes to other possible methods of collecting evidence.

On the other side of the argument to the positivists are the empiricists, who acknowledge that in reality what and how we come to know about the world is influenced by our own human experience of the world. An empiricist view is one in which theories can never be fully proven, and it is a view in which there is value in other approaches to data collection and analysis beyond the RCT, especially when you do not have access to large numbers of participants and the resources needed to run large trials. We instil in our participants an awareness of the need to acknowledge and manage the subjective aspects of their activities, to approach their methods with consistency and to ensure that they will be able to verify the research they design.

A second important issue for considering what makes evidence sound is the generalizability of research studies. Few of our entrepreneurs are in a position to conduct trials with large numbers of participants, or trials that last a very extensive amount of time. This means that generalizability is also likely to evade them. We therefore teach them about the value of transferability and the way in which they can justify the rigour of their studies by identifying that their research methods can be applied in a different setting. In order to do this, participants need to identify factors of sufficient similarity between the original setting and the setting to which transfer is proposed in order for transfer to be feasible.

The explicit target of our training activities is to help our entrepreneurs gather evidence that will help them to improve the design of their product or service and demonstrate to their investors and customers what their product or service can achieve. There is, however, another important reason why we provide this training: we want our entrepreneurs to be able to use existing evidence from previous research studies effectively. This means that we need them to be able to differentiate what is and is not good evidence. By helping them to understand what needs to be in place for data collection and analysis to be effective for addressing their particular intervention, we are also helping them to make judgements about the validity and value of the existing evidence that they can access. We want them to apply to the research reports and papers that they read the same questioning mindset they use in designing their own research studies. By using the knowledge and skills from our research training they should be able to select the most appropriate evidence and use it wisely to inform their educational technology intervention.

Back to intelligence, human and artificial

Before I leave this first chapter, I must return to its title: 'Intelligence, human and artificial'. I have written about my concern that we undervalue human intelligence. This occurs because we take for granted a great deal about human intelligence, including its roots in social interaction. We also disregard the need to understand what it means to know something, which is in fact essential in order to make wise decisions about what we know and what we should question. But what has this got to do with artificial intelligence? The connection is in fact important, because as mentioned above the methods we use for identifying, talking about and valuing human intelligence are impoverished. These impoverished methods lead us to underestimate our intelligence and overestimate the capacity of machine behaviour, which we consequently describe as intelligent – artificially intelligent. I want to seed in your mind right here in this first chapter the idea that you should question more closely the intelligence of artificial intelligence. In particular, you should question the ability of artificial intelligence to justify what it knows and believes.

In chapters 2 and 3, I unpack the various elements that are important in any consideration of human intelligence. I do this to persuade you that our intelligence is an incredible feat, rich and complex. I will illustrate that intelligence is rooted way beyond our ability to learn school subjects, to retain facts, to solve complex maths problems, to take great photographs or to write great essays, film scripts or poems. Intelligence is social, emotional, subjective, not always predictable but always available to reflection. I will show that self-awareness and self-efficacy are fundamentally important, and as yet unavailable to artificial machine-based systems.

In Chapter 3, I will move on to explain intelligence as found in the ways that we develop our knowledge about ourselves, as we go about our business in the world. I will explore how we develop an ability to know what we know and how we know it: metacognition. I will write about social interaction and social intelligence – a particularly undervalued element of human intelligent behaviour. I will also explain the importance of our subjective and physical experience of the world, because these are fundamental to how we come to know about the world as well as how we come to know about ourselves.

Chapter 4 integrates the elements of intelligence that I write about in chapters 2 and 3. I introduce the idea of **interwoven intelligence** as a way of thinking and talking about intelligence. Interwoven intelligence consists of seven different elements. I use the word *element* because it characterizes something that is essential and significant.

Chapter 5 explores the implications of this broader and richer appreciation of human intelligence for the way that we can and must relate to our artificial intelligences by invoking and valuing our much more complex human intelligence. Chapter 6 explains the implications of using AI to help humans to improve their intelligence. If we get our education systems right, we can use AI to help us to keep striving for intellectual growth. I focus on learning, and highlight that learning is the reason that artificial intelligence is now threatening us: that we need to remember artificial intelligence does not get tired of learning, and that the fact AI is always learning means it is always improving. We must therefore also accept that we must continually learn. Learning is the holy grail of success and intelligence. If we are good at learning, the world is our oyster and we can continually progress.

The final chapter pulls together its main argument and recounts the evidence that the six previous chapters have provided for my premise. To summarize, this is that the methods we use for identifying, talking about and valuing human intelligence are impoverished. As a consequence of these impoverished tools, we are dumbing down, not smarting-up, the most valuable resource in the world: ourselves. There are several means by which we can do more to value human intelligence, principally through the seven elements of interwoven intelligence. I focus in particular on epistemic cognition and perceived self-efficacy. Cultivating epistemic cognition can serve as a foil for my initial claim in the book that we are obsessed with measurement and are becoming incapable of making good judgements from a range of evidence sources. Fostering perceived self-efficacy, meanwhile, is the crucial factor for developing human intelligence and the key 'currency' we might want for our 'Fitbit for the mind', were it ever to be built.

Chapter 2

What is intelligence? Part 1: Knowledge and knowing the world

Intelligence is something that we celebrate, and something that we mock. It is something we believe that we all have to some extent, and we believe that we instinctively know what it is. We test it, and we compare who is more intelligent or less intelligent. Human intelligence is our intellectual capacity, our ability to construct knowledge and understanding as we interact in the world, to develop skills and expertise. Intelligence enables us to learn, to communicate, make decisions, express ourselves and interpret others. Our conceptions of intelligence have developed over the decades, but I question whether they have developed sufficiently to equip us to deal with the onslaught of intelligent machines.

There are numerous theories about intelligence. For example, at the start of the 20th century Charles Spearman (2005) proposed a theory of general intelligence that consisted of different types of intelligences that are correlated. Much more recently Howard Gardner (1983) has likewise proposed a theory of multiple intelligences, eight to be precise, with existential and moral intelligence being suggested latterly for possible inclusion. However, for Gardner there is no correlation between these different types of intelligence. Sternberg (1985) has a more limited set of multiple intelligences – namely analytic, creative and practical – in his triarchic theory of intelligence. These theories are all interesting and worthy of attention. However, my perspective here is specific to the challenge of recognizing and valuing intelligence in a way that is useful in helping us avoid reducing the value of our own intelligence to that which can currently be produced by artificially intelligent technology. I am not so concerned with the intricacies of how intelligence works, or in developing a theory to challenge those that already exist. I am interested in finding ways of talking about intelligence that enable us to get the best value out of our intelligence.

I have already indicated in Chapter 1 that human development, and the social basis of thought and consciousness, are important to how I perceive intelligence. The concepts of instincts and intuition have also been flagged, and here I will look in greater detail not just at the cognitive and metacognitive aspects of our intelligence, but also at the importance of our emotions and the embodied nature of intelligence. I want intelligence to be respected as the rich and complex essence of our humanity.

At this point, I must make clear that I know there are volumes of research, analysis, philosophy, comment and rhetoric about intelligence, written by people with a great deal of expertise from across multiple disciplines. My approach is pragmatic, and motivated by a desire to understand more about intelligence myself. I have read widely, and yet my knowledge about intelligence is still very incomplete. However, rather than allowing the inertia of my own ignorance to prevent me from addressing something that I care about deeply I have decided to embrace my inadequacies, because they mean that I am constantly questioning everything I confront that might increase my understanding of human intelligence. It is this constant questioning that I hope will make this book of value. And it is this constant willingness to question that I believe we must all embrace so that we can continually develop our human intelligence.

My quest for increased understanding leads me to try to unpack the key dimensions of intelligence. The unpacking task is the purpose of this chapter.

We talk with ease about whether or not we believe in something, whether or not something is true. These everyday conversations are markers of the way that knowledge has been conceived and theorized for thousands of years. I will pay considerable attention to our relationship with the ways that we talk about knowledge, from the original conceptualization of knowledge as 'justified true belief' at the time of Plato to what I hope will be an appreciation of the complexity of our relationship with knowledge, and the importance of understanding this relationship if we are to use our intelligence wisely. I will suggest that, in order to progress, it may be time to effect a paradigm shift in our conceptualizations of intelligence. I will propose that we need to think differently about intelligence if we are to outwit the smart machines that are coming our way. The idea of paradigm shift was suggested by the American philosopher Thomas Kuhn (1962), who used this phrase to describe the need for science to move beyond a linear and continuous way of progressing and for scientists to engage with their subjective experiences in order to move to intellectual spaces previously unthinkable. It is now time to engage our subjective self in the question of what intelligence is.

What is knowledge?

Let's start with something simpler than intelligence – something that is important to intelligence but that is not intelligence in and of itself. Let's talk about knowledge. The way that I talk about knowledge arises from my experiences with the world to date. These include, for example, my own experience of education, my experience of teaching learners of all ages, my studies within computer and cognitive science and in particular with artificial intelligence. These experiences have all influenced the way that I now think about knowledge. I am an interdisciplinary scholar and therefore my discussions will not have the depth of those generated by an expert philosopher or a dedicated epistemologist. They will, however, draw upon the multiple disciplines that I believe are fundamental to the way that we need to see knowledge in the 21st century. I hope that the way I scuff across the disciplines will produce the right material to meet my needs and that it may cause sufficient irritation to introduce other enquiring minds to explore the thoughts I offer in greater depth.

I am driven by a desire to find an appropriate way to talk about knowledge at a time when we are wallowing in data. We have in our pockets computing power that was merely a dream when I was studying undergraduate computer science more than 25 years ago, and we face an onslaught of artificially intelligent systems that are usurping us in the roles that we cherish as our human ground. I feel uneasy about the way that we currently talk about knowledge. I feel unnerved and disconcerted by the language we are using, because I know that it is not serving us well. We are cheapening the value of knowledge and confusing it with information, and I want to find a way to redeem its status and ensure that it is understood and valued in its broader sense.

I can pinpoint the precise moment, in January 2012, when my concern about knowledge surfaced to the extent that I knew I had to do something about it. It was a sunny morning and I was walking along the Euston Road in London, where I pass the British Library. A sign caught my eye: 'Step inside – Knowledge freely available'. This made me angry. I dislike the suggestion that one can walk into the British Library and just pick up some knowledge like going into a supermarket and buying some bananas. I know that I have to construct knowledge from the evidence available to me, that it is not handed to me by others, though they can certainly help me along the way. I also know that I aspire to increase my knowledge continually by weaving together the information resources distributed throughout my world. I know that this is hard work. The same month in which I saw this sign, I started a blog called *The Knowledge Illusion* to help me set out my concerns and engage others in discussions about them (Luckin, n.d.). When writing about the issues that worry me and my ideas about how to address them, many of which appear in this book, I know that these have evolved through the blog.

My own curiosity about knowledge started when I was eight years old and growing up in semi-detached suburbia: dad, mum, older brother and me. My father was an aircraft engineer and my mother taught typing and shorthand to women whose working lives were about to be transformed by the word processing power of the digital computer. My brother was three years older than me, and his lack of interest in formal education was causing my parents some concern. Our house was not exactly stuffed with books, but to my parents' credit their reaction was to invest in what they thought would be 'knowledge books'. They spent their very hard earned and rather meagre money on *A Children's Book of Knowledge* and an encyclopaedia. These volumes now filled up the bureau bookshelf. To keep us up to date, there was also the weekly general knowledge magazine that plopped on the doormat with a reassuring thud, the weight of its knowledge resounding clearly for all to hear.

My brother's reaction to the start of our own library was unenthusiastic: he was far more motivated by exploring the woodland around our housing estate than with sitting at home and reading about it. My father, however, became quite addicted to the weekly general knowledge magazine. He did not have a great deal of time to read, but each evening when he went to bed he would sit in his paisley pyjamas and thumb through the pages of these magazines. The stockpile of copies soon grew on the nightstand, as his pace of reading failed to match the frequency of their arrival. The corners became slightly curled as the months and years passed and the dust gathered in and around a pile that now extended from the nightstand to the floor. His interest, though, never waned and there was a pile of old issues by his bedside when he died many years later.

For my father, knowledge was something that he could find in the dusty pages of his out-of-date magazines. I do not share my father's belief that knowledge is something to be found in books or magazines. I do, however, believe that if one has the skills and abilities to construct knowledge effectively for oneself, the information that these books and magazines contain offers valuable ingredients for those constructions. I admire my father's quest for knowledge and I am sure that it has been a big influence on my own somewhat different expedition along this route.

The first encyclopedia to be published – the *Encyclopédie* – appeared during the Enlightenment, when leading intellectuals such as Voltaire and Denis Diderot met in the 18th century French salons. The *Encyclopédie* was a huge step in our intellectual development because its 35 volumes were exported to other parts of Europe, including England, and provided information about the world that we could, as Vygotsky would say, use like 'a tool'. The way we manipulated this tool helped us to learn in advanced and sophisticated ways. A social science perspective would portray the process of knowledge acquisition as one involving complex cognitive, experiential, association and reasoning processes. It involves strenuous mental efforts and engages our conscious mind. Knowledge, then, is not something I can acquire simply by walking into a library, picking up a book and reading text. Neither is knowledge homogeneous, as suggested in that British Library sign that made me so cross.

Not all forms of knowledge are equally available to our reasoning senses. If I access information about astrophysics I will find it much harder to construct a knowledgeable understanding of this subject than I will if I read a book about the Von Neumann architecture in computing. Our ability to construct a knowledgeable understanding is dependent upon our own existing understanding and it is influenced by the nature of different specialisms, some of which are more clearly defined and structured than others. Our knowledge is concerned with our relationship to the world, a world that is constantly changing and evolving and that demands we constantly evaluate our own relationship to it and what it means for us to know something about it. It is this propensity for knowledge construction that we use to make sense of the world; it sets us apart from other animals. It is the ingredients of knowledge that we represent and manipulate in the symbols of our language so that we can talk about knowledge in the abstract as well as in the particular of its situation.

Unlike the factual information that my father loved so much to study and memorize, knowledge is a far less straightforward concept than information. It has been the subject of heated debate over centuries, with many definitions and theories published and debate still raging today, with some philosophers and scientists devoting their lives to its study. In Europe, things were more clear-cut before the Enlightenment. However, thanks to thinkers like Locke, Spinoza and Newton, we were propelled into the age of reason and the promotion of intellectual exchange.

There is insufficient space here to engage in a historical or philosophical account of the study of knowledge. I do, however, want to offer a way of thinking and talking about knowledge that can help us to make useful differentiations between what is and what is not knowledge. This is increasingly important as we are faced with an abundance of potential candidates to become part of our knowledge in this digital age. My aim is to be informed by the most influential theories about knowledge and to find a way to fit them together, one that provides a useful way to talk about knowledge and intelligence now that we are dealing with 'intelligent' machines as well as intelligent people. I hope to demystify what is perhaps one of the most opaque areas of our intellectual heritage, to empower my readers, because I believe it is extremely important that more people are enabled to engage in thinking about knowledge and in understanding their own personal epistemologies.

Knowledge and belief

A useful and relatively straightforward first step is to differentiate knowledge from belief. I believe that Sean Connery is the best James Bond, although Daniel Craig pushes him to a close second. I also believe that the Dreamliner aircraft that flew me to New York last month is capable of staying in the air. However, this does not, in and of itself, mean that these beliefs equate to my knowledge. My views about James Bond are really just opinions, while my faith in the Dreamliner is based upon justifiable evidence and would indeed fit with Plato's definition of knowledge as *justified true belief*. Only my belief about the Dreamliner has the potential to be considered knowledge. The extent to which we can agree that it is knowledge will depend upon the definition of knowledge that we accept and the evidence that we use to demonstrate its truth.

My aim here is not to tell you what definition of knowledge you should adopt, but rather to suggest possibilities that you might like to consider, and to engage you in thinking about what you believe knowledge to be. I hope that this book will give you tools to think with as you try to distinguish the true from the false, to decide if there is sufficient evidence to enable you to accept that something should be added to your beliefs, and to differentiate among the information that you use to construct your evolving knowledgeable understanding of the world.

What does knowledge do for us?

As a useful second step after discussing beliefs as distinct from knowledge, we can immediately consider what knowledge does for us. It is fair to describe knowledge as the stuff that helps us to make sense of the world. But is it also fair to describe knowledge as being something that has some objective existence beyond our own experiences with the world, and beyond the experiences of others with the world?

I want the answer to this question to be yes, because this would enable me to give credence to the value of my own school studies. I remember biology lessons that involved boiling a green leaf to extract its chlorophyll as part of my learning about the role that plants play in animal respiration. I also remember that there is a formula for the process of photosynthesis that I had studied, and I am sure I could remember it if I tried. I am also sure that when I was at school studying this process, I believed this was a proven scientific process that had been discovered by experts and that it revealed a truth about the world with respect to respiration. I find it hard to contemplate how I might understand respiration without the belief that this formula is an objective truth with explanatory power. However, I also want to believe that our own experience of the world has value.

The tension between the objective and the subjective lies very much in the territory of Kahneman's work about the relationship between our experiential mind and our algorithmic mind, as discussed in Chapter 1. I want to believe, for instance, that a theory such as legitimate peripheral participation (Lave and Wenger, 1991) which suggests that one learns in a situated manner from and with a community, is an authentic basis for knowledge. In other words, I am attracted to the authenticity of post-modern thinking about the distributed, grounded nature of knowledge, but I also like the abstraction that scientific theories, such as that relating to respiration, offer us. I can understand respiration through its chemical formula and I have the experience of breathing in the world, thanks to the trees and plants that surround me. However, I am also well aware that the explanatory power offered by the scientific method can also be criticised for its lack of contextualization. As a student of all things that relate to context and a true believer in the paucity of our understanding of its importance within our education system, any lack of contextualization presents a big problem for me.

In Chapter 1 I described how, at University College London, we aim to engage the entrepreneurs we work with in thinking beyond the positivist assertions behind the experimental research methodologies to which they are naturally attracted. Positivism rears its head here too: it asserts that there exists some authentic knowledge that is objective and capable of positive verification. Lying at the heart of the scientific method that replaced the previously dominant metaphysics, positivism is grounded in a circular interdependence between theory and empirical research in science. It was also highly influential in the work of Émile Durkheim, who formulated the foundations of social research, which in turn were later rejected by the critical theorists who adopted an anti-positivist stance. However, for me positivism is wholly inadequate. Along with great thinkers like Karl Popper (1982), I accept that it is impossible to verify for sure that what I believe is true, because we will never be in possession of all the information required for authentic verification. It is, however, possible to demonstrate that some beliefs are false and not worthy of being called knowledge.

The possibility to demonstrate that something is false advances the solution to my dilemma concerning the nature of knowledge, but it is not an answer in and of itself. The post-positivism of Popper maintains the possibility that there is an objective truth. This is attractive, because it allows me to accept the scientific formulas I learnt at school as an objective truth, but it is at the same time a cause for concern because it is also a route through which authoritarian claims can be made on areas of knowledge. The monks of the 15th century acted as guardians of our early books, because they could read in an age of general illiteracy. In the same way, the rules and codes of a knowledge discipline, such as physics, history or biology, can be used as powerful tools for rejecting change, sticking with traditions and ignoring the needs of subordinate groups. This is the classic impasse between objectivity and subjectivity, between positivism in its many forms and the post-modernists, and it demonstrates that I am still trying to have my cake and to eat it.

I don't want to end up in a situation in which knowledge is only that which arises from my own and others' experience in the world, because this reduces knowledge to a group of knowers and to the standpoints that they adopt. This kind of view can be politically powerful, and yet it can also play against those subordinate groups that it intends to support because it takes away the framework that they could use to emancipate themselves. In parallel with this acknowledgement of the weaknesses of the post-modernist approach, it is also important to acknowledge the transformational role that science has played in society since the 16th century. Much knowledge, as well as our appreciation of the importance of knowledge, has emerged as a result of the practice of scientific communities. We now need to take a new transformational step as a result of the work that has been done by technological communities.

Social knowledge

A slightly different way of framing the differences between objectivity and subjectivity can be found in the relationship between theory and practice. In Chapter 1, I introduced the work of the Russian psychologist Lev

Vygotsky, who believed in the social foundation of human consciousness and development. When Vygotsky was formulating his ideas, he would have been living a rather spartan existence in the early days of post-revolutionary Russia. The austerity of Vygotsky's life was brought home to me early in my PhD studies when I was lucky enough to attend a conference in Geneva where Vygotsky's daughter was present. The organizers of the conference had set up a small room where there was a display of some of Vygotsky's possessions as provided by his daughter. I was very struck by the metal extensions that were applied to the pencils he used to write with, so that the pencil could be used right up to the very end when it would be too small to hold between his thumb and fingers. I marvelled at the pages of his writing that were written on both sides and then again in the spaces between the original lines of writing. I cannot believe but that the meagreness of these resources must have had an impact upon what Vygotsky thought and wrote. It is no small wonder then that he believed our ability to use language to engage in abstract thought was grounded in our early use of tools. He saw language as a tool for abstract thought, just as a pencil is a tool for writing. Through language we can communicate and interact socially; we can develop the communal practices through which the psychological tools that lead us to our individual thoughts and understanding can be developed. It is the human ability to use language to engage in abstract thought that sets us apart from more primitive animals.

So far, this sounds like a story that is going to take us along the route of knowledge as experience, both our own and that of others. The setting in which Vygotsky was working was after all one of Marxist philosophy, which tends to collapse knowledge into practice and truth into the consequences of this practice. However, Vygotsky differentiated between knowledge that one acquires through one's direct experience of the world and knowledge that one acquires by interacting with a more knowledgeable other. This latter knowledge is beyond our direct experience. He referred to our experiential knowledge as *everyday knowledge* and to the knowledge that we do not directly experience as our *scientific knowledge*. The word scientific here does not restrict knowledge to the domains of science; rather it is used to identify that this type of knowledge is formal and theoretical, it is knowledge that cannot be experienced directly in the world. It is the fodder of our algorithmic mind.

Both everyday and theoretical knowledge arise from social interaction. It is the history of social interactions that shape societies and communities, that shape their individual knowledge and the knowledge of their members. Knowledge and claims of truth are always therefore embedded in forms of life. Scientific concepts are independent from context. They are systematic, and separate from everyday activities. Reality, as reflected in consciousness and sensation – as reflected in the everyday – is different. The nature of the relationship between the two, between scientific and everyday, is dialectical. Both are therefore embedded in and related to each other in an ongoing process. Theory is developed within practice and all meanings are created in the public social domain and then internalized through a process of learning. These learning processes start with the language of the culture in which the learner is learning and then progress through the tacit everyday knowledge of that learner's experience to the theoretical codified knowledge that has been developed through that culture's practice.

Knowledge is located in the world and is the outcome of people *acting* in the world to transform it. The acquisition and transmission of knowledge is central to education. However, the shallow way in which we currently perceive and talk about knowledge in most education systems means that the knowledge built within individuals and groups through their education is inadequate for today's world. This is also one of the reasons why the worldwide web, which should represent a new Enlightenment, is in fact encouraging us to dumb ourselves down. At heart, the web encourages us to mistake *information* for *knowledge*. Undoubtedly, it enables valuable information and smart software to reach many parts of the world that were far beyond the influence of the first encyclopedias – however, because we fail to realize that it is merely 'a tool' that we must learn to manipulate in advanced and sophisticated ways, we are not making best use of what it has to offer. We are not on the road to the next Enlightenment and the age of intelligence.

In the next section I will investigate how we might correct this situation by developing a more sophisticated understanding of what constitutes knowledge.

Epistemic cognition and personal epistemology

I have often wondered about the motivation for my father's persistent engagement with his 'knowledge' magazines. He was a man who loved factual information and hated anything that involved uncertainty. He believed that any form of argumentation was rude and that emotions were things best not discussed lest they got in the way of absorbing his much-treasured facts. He was a kind man and a caring father, but his approach to life had been marred by the fact that he had been abandoned at birth, reclaimed a few years later by a mother who then subjected him to near fatal abuse. He had only survived thanks to the energies of the maternity nurse who had cared for him after the original abandonment. She rescued him from the grips of my gruesome grandmother. Who would want to discuss their emotions or embrace uncertainty after that kind of childhood?

In addition to his enthusiastic reading of his 'knowledge magazines', my father also loved to tinker. He would disappear into the garage at the side of our house for long periods of time and mend things. He had a remarkable skill for this mending activity and was surprisingly creative with some of his products, although incredibly slow. As a child, I thought he could mend anything and I carried much of this optimism into adulthood. I remember in particular a friend seeing me taking him a metal ironing board, one foot of which had sheered-off. She asked me how on earth he was going to fix that. I could not tell her how, but I just knew he would. A few weeks later I was proved correct when he arrived with the ironing board now sporting a beautifully carved new wooden foot, carefully inserted into the remains of the existing jagged (now smoothed) metal leg and lovingly painted the same colour as the metal. It lasted for two decades more and I hated throwing it away when it really was past any form of redemption.

What surprises me to this day is that my father's practical garage tinkering did not translate to a desire to tinker with the information he read, to knowingly and deliberately engage with his own process of knowledge construction. When it came to what he thought of as knowledge he wanted to learn it, as it was offered, by rote. He loved the reassurance of the authority in the books and encyclopaedias, because these were written by people who knew more than him and he was happy to take the information they provided with confidence and without question. Their text was sufficient evidence for him to feel that he knew what he could remember from it. This made him an excellent quiz team member, but a poor intellectual discussant. I realized only some years after his death that when my father was absorbed in his knowledge magazines, he was demonstrating what is formally referred to as an unsophisticated personal epistemology.

There are many ways in which researchers discuss our understanding of the nature of knowledge. The difference in the terminology they use often reflects a particular theoretical position. The terms *epistemic* and *epistemological* are used interchangeably, the one referring to knowledge and the other to a theory of knowledge. The term *epistemological belief* is concerned with people's beliefs about epistemology, and the term *epistemic cognition* is a generic term referring to people's understanding about the nature of knowledge. Epistemic cognition refers to our cognition about knowledge and implies some level of reflection on our part upon our thinking about knowledge. The term *personal epistemology* is an all-encompassing one used to refer to the fact that people have a theory about the nature of knowledge, even if they do not recognize it explicitly as a theory. Personal epistemology can be thought of as the way in which each of us understands what knowledge is and the way we think about how we come to know something. It is also sometimes referred to as our epistemic cognition. I shall use the terms *epistemic cognition* and *personal epistemology* almost interchangeably throughout the rest of this book.

Epistemic cognition and intelligence

Epistemic cognition is an important subject for discussion when talking about knowledge and intelligence, because it is core to our perception of what it means to know and to understand something. It is fundamental to our conceptions of intelligence. One should not be surprised that there has been considerable discussion among philosophers and scientists about the nature of knowledge in an educational context, nor that there has been little agreement. However, there are some key aspects to this discussion that are relevant here. These relate to how we characterize students' conceptualizations of the nature of knowledge, to how we evaluate the adequacy of someone's knowledgeable understanding and to how we believe an understanding about the nature of knowledge should be part of our education system.

Could it be acceptable to allow our students to consider that there is some objective reality that is knowledge, because it can act as a stepping stone to more sophisticated understanding? Or should we insist from the outset that knowledge is only ever tentative?

Several years of teaching programming to undergraduate students taught me that sometimes one has to disguise the complexity of something in order to help people grasp those first few threads of understanding that will propel them into a position where they can cope with something more complex. I therefore concur with the theoretical frameworks of epistemic cognition formulated to date, and attend to simplifying the philosophical issues about the nature of knowledge.

In a few pages I will discuss cognition, metacognition and motivation, and it is useful therefore to situate this discussion of epistemic cognition as it relates to these other cognitive constructs, all of which are important to the way we think and talk about both knowledge and intelligence. Epistemic cognition should be considered as distinct from, but related to, the way we think about cognition, metacognition and motivation. For example, if I believe that my *cognitive* development is reflected in my ability to perform particular arithmetic procedures, and to reiterate what I have learnt through reading and study, then it is perfectly plausible that I might conceive of *knowledge* as consisting of noble facts rather than something that is open to interpretation and context-specific. Likewise, if we accept *metacognition* as something that would include my ability to monitor the extent to which I have successfully learnt something by conducting an arithmetic procedure, and I see knowledge as something that is objectively true, then I am more likely to overestimate the extent to which I understand arithmetic.

When it comes to motivation, work completed by Carole Dweck (2006) and her colleagues over the last few decades provides invaluable information. Although Dweck is popularly associated with the growth mindset, I came across her earlier work about goal orientation some years ago (Dweck, 1986; Elliot and Dweck, 1988). As a consequence, it is clear to me that students whose orientation at a particular moment is towards their performance in comparison to their peers are likely to hold a more simplistic view about the nature of knowledge than students who seek mastery without caring about how they perform in comparison to others.

The issue of epistemic cognition has been studied across the areas of psychology and education, as well as philosophy. The work of psychologists has looked across multiple subject areas, but the work within education has tended to focus upon science education. A seminal piece of work conducted by William Perry with Harvard undergraduate students in the mid-1950s highlighted the importance of our personal epistemology. This work outlined nine different positions that people could adopt towards the nature of knowledge. These nine positions ranged from a naïve understanding, in which the individual saw knowledge as being derived from authority, to a sophisticated understanding in which an individual believed that knowledge is self-constructed, relative to context and informed by an evidence base. Research evidence demonstrates that most people have a fairly unsophisticated personal epistemology. I believe that this hampers us as we grapple with the complexities of what is and is not intelligence in both humans and machines.

My own interest in personal epistemology was piqued by a particularly able PhD student, Katerina Avramides (2009), who produced a thesis exploring the role that technology could play in helping students to develop sophisticated epistemic cognition when studying ill-defined subjects and problems. She demonstrated to me the importance of a sophisticated personal epistemology, and her work is therefore a key element of my discussions in this chapter. Researchers and philosophers do not agree about the nature of knowledge and its development. My aim for this book is to provide a practical exposition of intelligence. This chapter is concerned with our construction of a knowledgeable understanding of the world, because knowledge is a key element of intelligence. I therefore limit my discussion of personal epistemology, or the process through which we justify that something is knowledge, to the way that personal epistemology impacts upon our knowledgeable understanding and the way we develop a more sophisticated grasp of the world. I therefore discuss work conducted within psychology and education.

Can we measure someone's epistemic cognition?

Research into epistemic cognition has produced a set of widely differing propositions, both conceptually and methodologically. Marlene Schommer-Aikins (2004) developed the multi-dimensional framework of epistemic cognition that today dominates in educational psychology. This framework is quantitative, in contrast to earlier qualitative developmental models. The framework offers a five-dimensional model that encompasses our beliefs about the nature of knowledge, our control of knowledge acquisition and the speed at which we acquire knowledge. Epistemic cognition is something that varies, not just between subject areas but within a single subject too.

However, as Avramides astutely pointed out, the assumptions that people's thinking complexity can be described through a set of dimensions, and that this can be captured in quantitative terms, have never been justified by Schommer-Aikins, either theoretically or empirically. They must therefore be considered as doubtful. Another area of concern is her use of questionnaires to collect the data upon which the measurements of people's epistemic cognition were proposed. One of the criticisms to which questionnaires are always susceptible is that one can never be sure that respondents have understood the questions in the way that questionnaire's designer intended.

Take, for example, the following statement: 'Learning definitions word for word is often necessary to do well on tests'. A positive response to this statement was evaluated by Schommer-Aikins as evidence of naïve epistemic cognition. And yet it is absolutely the case that in order to pass some exams all you need to do is learn definitions word for word. We should therefore treat the results of these questionnaire-based studies with caution (DeBacker *et al.*, 2008).

Can we describe different types of epistemic cognition?

Perhaps we can learn something more from the early developmental models of epistemic cognition? These models were criticised for their qualitative approach, but nevertheless they may contain something valuable for my purposes. The foundational work done by William Perry at Harvard University in the 1950s and 1960s revealed that, while some students were already comfortable with the idea that knowledge could be relative and tentative, others were equally comfortable with the idea that knowledge is absolute. Perry's interview-based qualitative methodology has been further developed by many researchers who followed his approach to collecting data (Belenky *et al.*, 1986; Baxter Magolda, 1992; Baxter Magolda and Porterfield, 1988). These subsequent researchers have also redressed the lack of diversity among Perry's student participants, who were all male and at Harvard.

For example, Baxter Magolda (1992) and her colleagues conducted a study that ran over 12 years with adults aged between 18 and 34. She used the data she collected during this time to develop a model of *epistemological reflection* that focused on people's ability to make meaning from their experiences based on their assumptions, and their context. Her model provides a developmental sequence of *patterns of thinking*. These patterns are described as:

- *absolute knowing,* which reflects people's belief that knowledge is certain and is provided by authority
- *transitional knowing,* a pattern that reflects a belief that some knowledge is uncertain but some other knowledge can be viewed as true
- *independent knowing,* a pattern in which individuals no longer believe in knowledge as absolute truth and see their own personal opinions as valid
- *contextual knowing,* the pattern for participants who realize that knowledge is context-dependent and that different viewpoints must be evaluated in order to reach a conclusion about any particular knowledge within its context.

Baxter Magolda (2004) subsequently revised the framework a little to recognize the substantial gender differences that she discovered in her data. She created subdivisions for each of the first three of her patterns. For example, she extended the absolute knowing pattern with a *received* and a *mastery* category. The *received absolute knowing* pattern was mostly applicable to women and was characterized by a focus on recording what they heard or read in order to acquire knowledge. The *mastery absolute knowing* pattern, mainly expressed by men, was illustrated by a propensity to get actively involved in trying to remember the material they read or heard.

Over the years, various models have described the way in which we develop our epistemic cognition through various stages of sophistication as we develop intellectually. The descriptions used by Baxter Magolda for her patterns of thinking were *absolute knowing, transitional knowing, independent knowing* and *contextual knowing*. Other models may have different numbers of stages and they may use different terminology, but they all track our progress as being from seeing knowledge as something absolute, certain and provided by some authority to perceiving it as something that we have to work at, something tentative, in need of justification and contextualized.

For example, Belenky developed a five-stage model describing modes of *silence, received knowing, subjectivism, procedural knowing* and *constructed knowing*. King and Kitchener (2002) proposed a rather complicated three-level, seven-stage developmental model of epistemic cognition: level 1, *pre-reflective thinking*, encompasses stages 1 to 3; level 3, *quasi-reflective thinking*, includes stages 4 and 5; level 3, *reflective thinking*, is the home for stages 6 and 7. And Deanna Kuhn (2001), whose research focused on argumentation, formulated three ways in which people could view knowledge: people could be *absolutists, multiplists* or *evaluativists*. Epistemological development within Kuhn's framework is described in terms of how an individual perceives the relationship between their subjective and objective views of knowledge. When we are at the level of the *realist* or the *absolutist* we see knowledge objectively; when we reach the *multiplicity* level we perceive knowledge in subjective terms; when we reach the level of the *evaluativist* our objective and subjective dimensions are co-ordinated. Subsequent research conducted by Kuhn and Weinstock (2002) has finessed this work with further detail and subdivisions, but the essence remains.

In contrast to the majority of the research in psychology, the knowledge and knowing model developed by Hofer and Pintrich (1997; 2002) did not try to measure epistemic cognition. Their model has four dimensions split across two general areas. Area 1 is described as concerning the *nature of knowledge* and has two dimensions: the first refers to the certainty of a person's knowledge, and the second refers to the simplicity of their knowledge. The lower levels of the certainty dimension represent those who believe that there is an absolute truth that exists with certainty; the higher levels reflect attitudes that depict knowledge as something tentative and evolving. The simplicity dimension reflects at its lower levels the view that knowledge is a set of noble facts, while at the higher levels knowledge is conceived as something that is relative and contextual. Area 2 of the Hofer and Pintrich theory is about the *nature of knowing*. Once again there are two dimensions: the first concerns the source of someone's knowledge and the second concerns the justifications individuals have for believing that they know something. The lower levels of the source-of-knowing dimension reflect someone who sees knowledge as coming from an external authority; the higher levels describe people who see the source of knowledge as themselves, as they develop their ability to construct knowledge through their interactions in the world. The lower levels of the justification dimension are used to describe people who accept the opinion of others without requiring evidence to justify these opinions; the higher levels of this dimension are reserved for those who know how to evaluate evidence and to substantiate the justification of their beliefs that they know something. These dimensions are described as developing in parallel, leading to a discussion of epistemic cognition in terms of an individual having an epistemological theory that is stable between and within contexts.

At the risk of oversimplification, this theory of epistemic cognition, while useful, still feels inadequate. It suggests that an individual can be described purely in terms of whether they view knowledge as certain and simple or evolving and contextual, combined with their views about whether knowledge comes from someone else and is to be believed without question, or is something that one constructs through strenuous mental effort and that requires substantiation with evidence.

How can all this research about epistemic cognition help us understand intelligence? I am persuaded that all the models I have discussed are evidence-based, and a substantial amount of data has been used in their formulation. However, I still feel dissatisfied. All the models suggest that we go through a sequence of qualitatively different ways of thinking about knowledge as our sophistication develops. They all also make the assumption that our epistemic cognition is coherent and that it is consistent across different contexts. Therefore, people can be described via these models as being in a particular stage of epistemic cognition. In reality, however, few of us are very consistent. We can hold radically different views about whether a particular knowledge claim is simple, certain or uncertain. There is also evidence that our epistemic cognition can be incoherent.

In Chapter 5, I will use the idea of sophisticated personal epistemology to discuss how we might better develop our education systems for and beyond the 21st century. I therefore need a good way to talk about epistemic cognition that will be fit for this purpose. So far, none of the models or frameworks discussed is fit for my purpose.

There is a growing body of evidence (Buehl and Alexander, 2006; Elby and Hammer, 2001; Hammer and Elby, 2002; Hammer *et al.*, 2005) that concurs with my dissatisfaction with the models and frameworks for epistemic cognition that I have discussed so far. This evidence can be summarized as follows:

- *Epistemic cognition varies for the same person across different subject areas and it is not coherent.* We know that we are not always the sophisticated, rational individuals that we like to think that we are. We are perfectly capable of holding two diametrically opposed beliefs and our epistemic cognition is likely to be anything other than coherent. The way that we theorize our epistemic cognition needs to be far more sophisticated if it is to encompass our own fallibility.
- *People's epistemic cognition varies between contexts.* This is not surprising because there is no single view about the nature of knowledge that applies across every context.
- *The dimensions postulated in a range of theories are hard to justify.*

My search for a model, or a framework, of epistemic cognition has not yielded an 'off-the-shelf' solution. I am therefore going to have to use this excellent evidence to formulate my own way of talking about and using epistemic cognition for the purposes of ensuring that it makes a contribution to the way I think about intelligence.

I know that knowledge and epistemology are important for my purposes. For example, I need a good way to talk about knowledge and epistemology to deal with today's technology. The times of my childhood were simple when it came to information. The information that was available to us came from more knowledgeable others, publications that one either bought or borrowed from the library, or – increasingly – from the television. The technological masterpiece of the world wide web was probably not even a glint in the eye of its inventor Tim Berners-Lee, then a teenager. The sheer abundance of the information now available through the world wide web throws into sharp relief how we see the relationship between information and knowledge: we confuse them for each other in the same way as that sign outside the British Library did in 2012. Our understanding of what knowledge is and what it means to know something has not progressed in tandem with this technological progress. This puts us at risk of succumbing to the illusion that we know more than we actually do, because the more information we have the more we become certain that we know something (Fisher *et al.*, 2015).

I was worried when I first saw that British Library sign that we were at risk of dumbing ourselves down through our belief that information was knowledge. My concern was that if we did not help people to understand what knowledge is and how it is different from information, then humans would not be progressing from the well-meaning but limited way of thinking about knowledge that was promoted in the books and magazines of my childhood. This concern has grown significantly along with the proliferation of artificially intelligent (AI) systems in everyday life in the technologically developed world. We interact with AI through its many practical applications in computers that have visual capabilities, that can learn, solve problems, make plans and understand (and produce) natural language, both spoken and written. These AI applications are now commonplace for tasks such as medical diagnosis, language translation, face recognition, autonomous vehicle design and robotics. On that day in January 2012, standing outside the British Library, I was concerned that at a time of information plenty we were at risk of having a knowledge famine. I am no less concerned now, and I am convinced that we need not only to unpack what we understand knowledge to be, but also to focus on developing more sophisticated personal epistemologies.

Summary

I have in this second chapter explored two elements of our human intelligence: knowledge and our relationship to it. My perspective has been less concerned with the intricacies of how intelligence works. It has been focused instead on the challenge of recognizing and valuing intelligence in a way that helps to avoid reducing the value of our own intelligence to that which can currently be produced by AI technology.

I have raised concerns that while the acquisition and transmission of knowledge are central to education, the currently inadequate ways in which most people talk and think about knowledge, including within education, mean that the knowledge that is built within people as a result is inadequate for our current purposes. We all too often confuse information for knowledge. Most people have a fairly unsophisticated personal epistemology. This is holding them back and is going to disadvantage us as we struggle to understand the complexities and consequences of what is and is not intelligence in both humans and machines. In addition to lacking sophistication, few of us are very consistent and coherent in our beliefs, our knowledge and our certainty about how and what we know. And yet we have the capacity to be sophisticated and coherent in our self-knowledge and understanding. AI does not even have the capacity for the sophistication of epistemic cognition that we should all be aiming to achieve, if we want to remain distinctly intelligent.

I have taken some time to explain why it is not only important for us to construct a knowledgeable understanding of the world around us, but also to have a good understanding of what counts as knowledge, how certain knowledge can be, the extent to which knowledge is grounded in our context, and how we can hold inconsistent and different views about knowledge all at the same time. I have concluded that I cannot simply integrate any of the existing models of epistemic cognition into the way I think and discuss intelligence, although I can of course be strongly influenced and informed by this wealth of existing research.

In the next chapter I will unpack more about human intelligence. I will focus in particular on meta-level intelligence, because this meta-level is fundamental to our knowledge about ourselves. It is our ability to develop a sophisticated knowledge and understanding of our own abilities, emotions, experiences, knowledge and skills, and personal context that sets us aside from AI. These abilities are therefore extremely important.

Chapter 3

What is intelligence? Part 2: Knowledge of and knowing about ourselves

In Chapter 2, we saw that existing models of epistemic cognition are based on sound research, but none of them explain our propensity to lack consistency and sophistication. So how can we better develop the sophistication of our knowing about knowing, as well as our knowing about knowledge?

In this chapter we will move on to look at meta-level intelligence – our intelligence about ourselves – to help unpack human intelligence more effectively. I feel sure that this knowing about ourselves is fundamental to our intelligence, to increasing the sophistication of our knowledge of the world and to the way we think about what knowledge is and how we come to know something.

Intelligence is more than our knowledgeable understanding about the world, although such understanding is an important aspect of our intelligence. One of the things that humans are capable of developing is a knowledge of their own knowledge and thinking, a knowledge about how they are feeling, a knowledge of their personal context. This self-knowledge takes us beyond cognition into the realms of meta-level thinking. But let's start with cognition.

Cognition

In simplistic terms cognition is the process of thought through which we develop our knowledge and understanding of the world. It encompasses both our experiential and our algorithmic minds, and requires us to engage our attention, our memory, our problem-solving and our evaluation abilities. Our cognitive development is the way in which we increase our ability to construct knowledge and understanding as we interact in the world. Cognition is what we often confuse with intelligence, and the results of cognition are what most artificial intelligence (AI) systems deliver. We now need to look more determinedly beyond cognition to the way humans can develop knowledge and understanding of themselves and of their cognition, in addition to their knowledge and understanding of the world.

Metacognition

Our ability to know and regulate our own thinking has been a topic of discussion since at least the time of Aristotle, who was concerned about our awareness of our own thinking. This fascination with our relationship to our own mental processes, a phenomenon now referred to frequently as *metacognition*, has grown into a substantial area of study. Countless empirical studies have shown that metacognition is a key component of the way in which successful people operate in the world. However, our awareness of our own thinking and our ability to regulate our mental processes are rarely explicitly evaluated through the assessment practices of most education systems.

In my previous discussions of the work of the Russian psychologist Lev Vygotsky, I have said little about the extent to which people are aware of their own mental functions. The term metacognition was not in use at the time of Vygotsky's work, and yet mental self-awareness is an area on which Piaget and Vygotsky are, unusually, in agreement. Piaget looked at how children think and construct their own view of the world. He suggested that children work through various stages to help construct meaning and that they need to make things to help them understand how things work (Boden, 1980). Both men recognized that people, specifically young people or children, lack awareness of their mental functions. There was, even early in the 20th century, agreement between these icons of psychology that we needed to develop this awareness of our mental functions in order to develop the sophistication of our intellect.

The word metacognition, however, was not introduced until the 1970s by John Flavell (1979). The concept has undergone much refinement and its complexity is summarized well in a 2011 book by Pina Tarricone (2011), who has investigated the psychology literature about metacognition thoroughly and has produced an excellent taxonomy of metacognition. Her tabulated version of this taxonomy has seven tables that extend over some 20 pages of her book. However, despite the size of the subject, the term *metacognition* can be defined, broadly, as *our knowledge and control of our own cognitive processes.*

Tarricone recognizes the work of earlier researchers like Flavell (1979), and further differentiates between our knowledge of our cognitive processes and the processes that we use to monitor and regulate them. The latter include the executive functions of planning, mental resource allocation, monitoring, checking, error detection and correction, for example. She differentiates between our:

- knowing about our knowing, which she describes as *declarative metacognitive knowledge*
- knowing how to know, or our *procedural metacognitive knowledge*
- knowing when, where and why to know, or our *conditional metacognitive knowledge*.

When it comes to the skills to regulate our knowledge and our executive functioning, Tarricone distinguishes our *ability to monitor and control the knowledge we use* to solve a task, and the strategies we apply to this task, from our *metacognitive experiences*, which include our knowledge of our feelings and our judgements.

At around the same time that Tarricone was working on her thesis in Australia, I was working with colleagues at the University of Sussex on a much more modest enterprise to develop a conceptual framework for metacognition, motivation and emotions. This work was led by Ben du Boulay and had the purpose of informing the design and use of adaptive educational technologies – or, as we described them, systems that care (du Boulay *et al.*, 2010). Both Tarricone and the team at Sussex were citing many of the same research studies, and yet we were unaware of each other's work because we were working on opposite sides of the globe and in different disciplines. We were publishing at almost the same time, but at different conferences and in different journals. Our work was more or less hidden from each other.

The framework we developed at Sussex is not a taxonomy and our language is sometimes different to that used by Tarricone, but we cover much of the same territory. The section of our framework that deals with metacognition is tiny in comparison to Tarricone's taxonomy. However, much of what Tarricone includes within her conceptualization of metacognition we include within the other parts of our framework. We saw metacognition as our ability to articulate and regulate the mental processes that we use to construct our knowledge, understanding and skills. We identified context and metacontext to describe the physical, social and temporal setting in which a person is learning, and their ability to articulate their understanding of this context and to regulate it. We also identified motivation and metamotivation; emotion and meta-affect. We used motivation to describe a person's drive for learning and their understanding of why they are learning and what they hope to achieve. The metamotivation category was used to describe someone's ability to articulate and regulate this motivation. Our affect and meta-affect categories were included to describe a person's emotions with respect to learning, along with their ability to articulate and regulate these emotions. Our final additional category was that of a person's physiological and metaphysiological cognition, which we used to describe the bodily experiences that provide evidence relevant to learning. For example, there is a relationship between our heart rates and our facial expressions, and there is an extent to which we are able to articulate and regulate these physical processes.

The main differences in what Tarricone included in her extensive taxonomy and what we included in our more modest framework can be found in our inclusion of context and physiology. There are references to context within the Tarricone taxonomy, for example task context and strategy context. They are, however, in the detail rather than acknowledged as categories in their own right. Physiology is not included. By contrast, we do not specifically include judgement in our framework, whereas Tarricone does. This is not because we did not believe it to be important, but rather because we believe it to be beyond the scope and purpose of our framework. On reflection, I think this was probably a mistake. I think we should have included within our framework something relating to judgement and epistemic cognition. This is something I will tackle in greater detail later, because I have come to realize that we need our epistemic cognition to develop along with our metacognitive knowledge and skills in order to develop our self-efficacy. And we need our self-efficacy to develop and prosper as lifelong learners in a world increasingly augmented with artificially intelligent systems. I am now sure that we had better have a clear understanding about our own relationship to what knowledge is and how we make judgements about it, as well as a knowledge of our thinking and an ability to regulate it.

Sophisticated metacognition is important for intellectual development and for our performance in school and beyond. People who develop good self-regulation skills are more likely to fulfil their potential and achieve, for example. And there is good evidence that self-regulation skills have important benefits for learning and attainment, and that there is a positive relationship between self-regulation and academic achievement. We also know that self-regulation exists independently of prior attainment.

Metacognitive knowledge and skills can be developed and improved with appropriate teaching and support. Self-regulation can be improved through appropriate guidance and the creation of supportive and challenging learning environments. The early years are important for the development of the foundations of self-regulation, such as attention, inhibition and working memory. These can then be further developed through the later years and adolescence, so that self-regulation becomes more skilful and directed towards complex problem-solving.

A key aspect of self-regulation in older learners is the development and use of appropriate learning strategies. Older learners should be encouraged to develop, modify and reflect on their own methods to promote a greater understanding and better links between understanding and attainment. Self-regulation provides an organizing framework for exploring relationships between skills, attitudes and processes that are integral to effective learning.

Many scholars have explored the relationship between metacognition and our intellectual performance. Jerome Bruner (1996), for example, described the way in which our metacognitive awareness can enhance processes such as attention, problem-solving and intelligence. Scholars such as Marzano (1998) have demonstrated that our metacognitive skills and abilities can benefit the learning outcomes that we measure in our education system. Goos and her colleagues (2002) have given us the evidence that successful students are continually evaluating, planning and regulating their progress, thus helping them to learn and to develop their deep-level processing. We also know that the development of executive metacognitive processes is associated with enhanced cognitive performance.

Metacognition, as we have seen, involves our interpretation of our ongoing mental activity, and these interpretations are grounded in our interactions with the world beyond. However, metacognition also involves the interpretation of ongoing activity and the way that we make judgements based upon these interpretations of our interactions, using a whole host of contextualized cues. However, as Kornell (2009: 12) put it so succinctly, metacognition is not a case of 'turning an inward eye on [one's] memories and somehow analyzing them directly'. To believe that reflection in and of itself is sufficient for metacognition is to fail to appreciate the sophistication of our metacognitive processing.

Our metacognition is not failsafe, and even among those of us with well-developed metacognitive skills and abilities there is substantial evidence that learners draw faulty inferences from their experiences. For example, a paper by Wolfe and Williams (2017) demonstrates how little aware people can be that their knowledge and beliefs about something have been changed through their interactions in the world. This research was based on the premise that we change our beliefs as we acquire new evidence relevant to these beliefs. The goal of these authors' work was to examine the extent to which people were aware that their beliefs were changing as they encountered different pieces of relevant evidence. Their work was conducted with undergraduate psychology students. In two experiments, student participants reported their beliefs about the effectiveness of spanking as a means of disciplining children. The students were divided into two groups and were then asked to read a one-sided text about spanking and discipline. One group of students was asked to read a text that was consistent with the beliefs they had reported before reading, and the other group of students was asked to read text that reflected a position inconsistent with their reported beliefs. After reading, students were asked about their beliefs again. Students who read a text that was inconsistent with their reported beliefs were more likely to change their beliefs than those students who read a text that was consistent with their reported initial beliefs. The results from these studies demonstrated that students changed their beliefs more when they were asked to read new evidence that was inconsistent with their initial beliefs. This seems unsurprising, but the really interesting findings concern the extent to which students were aware that their beliefs had changed. In addition to being asked about their beliefs after reading the texts, the students were also asked after reading to recollect what they had believed before reading the text. Students' recollections of their initial beliefs tended to be biased in the direction of their new, post-reading current beliefs. These students now made large recollection errors when attempting to recall their initial beliefs. There was no evidence that the type or the duration of processing in which students engaged to comprehend the new evidence made any difference to the accuracy of their recollections on their initial beliefs.

To summarize, the students who read new evidence that did not concur with their previous beliefs were subject to belief change, and reported recollections of their initial beliefs that were in fact closer to the values of their current beliefs. The direction and extent of this belief change was related to the accuracy with which these students recalled their initial beliefs. I suspect that there is also a strong element of poor epistemic cognition at play in the phenomenon reported. Epistemic cognition, as we have seen, is an extremely important facility. However, putting this suspicion aside for one moment, these results are extremely worrying and they are certainly consistent with recent reports about how social media has manipulated people's opinions of electoral candidates in the USA and the UK (see, for example, Hern, 2017; Earle, 2017).

It is not surprising that the students who took part in Wolfe and Williams's studies changed their beliefs in the light of new scientific evidence. This is after all what we expect. Admittedly, we would also hope that students would be rigorous in their questioning of the validity of the evidence with which they were being presented, and mindful of its relationship to the evidence that they had previously encountered and interpreted to form their initial beliefs. But the change in beliefs is not, in and of itself, necessarily worrying. The evidence from this study that demonstrates the bias in people's memories about the beliefs they held before being confronted by new scientific evidence is, however, more worrying. And the really worrying feature in this study's results is that the students who took part were unaware that their beliefs had changed.

Wolfe and Williams assert that our conceptions about how our beliefs have or have not changed is a metacognitive function. They suggest that recalling our previous beliefs is a difficult task, something much harder than forming a judgement about a belief by reading some scientific evidence. For us to recall our previous beliefs after a period in which we have faced alternative and fresh evidence, we would need to be able to reconstruct the results of our mental processing at a previous time. This reconstructive process is something that is unfamiliar to us, and we are conversely terrifically good at post hoc rationalizations, and at telling ourselves a convincing story about what we thought and believed at a previous time. The situation is complicated by the fact that our previous beliefs may have been formulated over a long period of time, across multiple experiences and may have resulted from encountering a variety of different evidence sources. Put another way, our beliefs are heavily contextualized rather than stable components of our long-term memory. We therefore remember them incorrectly. Alternatively, it may simply be that we like to believe that we hold a stable position – after all, stable is what our algorithmic minds should surely make us. We therefore assume that our initial beliefs were very much in line with those that we hold now; anything else would challenge our perceptions of our stability.

Similar findings have been identified in studies conducted to evaluate the extent to which people's attitudes change in the light of new evidence, and the extent to which we are aware of these changes. So, how should those of us involved in the public discussion about science react to these findings? If we make people more aware of their vulnerability and that they are having their beliefs changed in a way about which they are unaware, will they be less willing to engage with material that is inconsistent with their current belief systems? If people do open themselves up to the possibility of alternative beliefs, and read fresh evidence, will this make them more vigilant about the extent to which they allow this evidence to change their beliefs? I would suggest that the latter is a healthy attitude to adopt and that it is an attitude associated with a more sophisticated epistemic cognition. This makes clear that developing a sophisticated personal epistemology is essential for human intelligence as we now need to conceive of it.

I hope that this text about metacognition has awakened your senses to the subject's complexity. Our metacognitive strategies are not processes that we automatically or naturally apply spontaneously and accurately across all subject areas, in all environments, or with all our peers and mentors. Metacognition in all its glory is something that must be learnt, developed, encouraged and supported. This is a subject we will return to in Chapter 5.

Emotions and motivation

Within the psychological sciences there are libraries full of books about human emotions. For the purposes of this book I'm constraining my discussion of emotions to those that relate to our feelings about learning and our motivation to learn. It is these emotions that I believe are fundamentally part of our human intelligence.

There is a substantial body of evidence that demonstrates the importance of the way we feel to how we learn. This evidence comes from across the social and psychological sciences, and now from within neuroscience. Our talk about our feelings, as researchers, uses a variety of terminology; most notably for my purposes a person's emotional state is often referred to as their *affective state*. Here I will use the terms *affect* and *emotion* interchangeably. As one might expect, there are a substantial number of theories about how our emotions affect whether, when and how we learn. For example, in the 1980s, Ortony and his colleagues (1988) came up with a theory that has been popular with researchers in the learning sciences. Ortony's team saw emotions in purely cognitive terms, as functions determined by someone's goals and attitudes. This assumes, of course, that the achievement of a goal is something that is important to us, which is in fact oversimplistic. Similarly, in the 1990s, Lazarus (1991) connected one's emotions to one's goals. He also saw additional influences in our potential for coping and our perceptions of the benefits of a particular activity to our well-being. There seems little doubt to me, however, that our emotions in relation to learning are far more complex than can be explained by our goals and attitudes.

Between 2007 and 2009, work conducted by Madeline Balaam (2009) while studying for her PhD at the University of Sussex illustrated the contextual nature of a group of students' emotions towards learning. Balaam was interested in how language-learning classrooms affected the emotional experiences of teenage learners. She was interested in the impact of emotions on each particular learning task, and she was interested in the impact of the learning environment on learners' emotions.

Balaam used an intriguing approach to ascertain the emotional states of her teenage learners: she equipped learners with a small juggling ball that had been adapted with wireless technology and that could be squeezed in order to change its colour. Each learner decided which of a selection of emotions was associated with each colour, and then squeezed the ball in order to turn its colour to that which represented the emotion they were experiencing at any particular moment. Because each student had selected their own colour/emotion mapping, anyone observing a student squeezing their ball to select a particular colour did not know what that colour meant in terms of that particular student's emotions. However, the wireless connection in the learner's coloured ball, and a little program code, meant that the data sent to the class teacher's tablet computer and to Balaam's hard drive conveyed a consistent view of the emotions of every learner and the changes to these emotions over time. Students were also asked to keep a diary about how they were feeling throughout the day. Balaam's research illustrated that the wider school setting and the classroom environment in which the learning task had been completed had a strong impact on each learner's emotions towards learning.

Much of the work that has explored the relationship between our emotions and our learning has focused on motivation. Motivation is a particular instance of the way in which our emotions impact upon our actions; indeed our actions impact too upon our motivation. It is the way that our emotions drive our actions to increase our knowledge and understanding of the world through our learning that is the focus of my attention here.

Theories of motivation

When we talk about motivation what do we mean? Are we referring to some physiological process that influences our desire to behave in a particular way, or are we merely referring to the reasons why we do something (Bergin *et al.*, 1993; Ryan and Deci, 2000)? Do we want to measure in some quantitative way the strength or extent of our motivation, or do we merely want to describe what influences us in completing particular actions? There are theories that can help us answer both these questions.

In a mammoth piece of work at the start of the 21st century, Pintrich (2000a) attempted to integrate the research about our motivation to learn. His work tries to incorporate a variety of theories about motivation and in doing so he identified three core components that he found across all the theories he explored.

First, Pintrich identified what he calls an *expectancy component* to motivation, which is concerned with our beliefs about our ability to complete a learning action. This expectancy component can be broadly subdivided into our beliefs about the extent to which we have control over the outcomes of a learning action and its environment, and beliefs about how effective we are likely to be if we attempt to complete the proposed learning action.

The second component Pintrich described is the *value component;* this refers to our beliefs about the value of the learning action under consideration. It reflects our perceptions of the importance of the learning action that will be influenced by our personal interest in the learning action and our perceptions of its utility for the future.

Third and finally there is the *affective component*, which accounts for our emotional or affective reactions to the learning action in question. This is particularly complex. It is not the case that being in a positive motivational state will necessarily increase our inclination to complete a particular learning action.

The three components of motivation in Pintrich's integrated theory are interconnected, and therefore our expectations about our performance, and the value we attribute to the particular learning action under consideration, will temper the way in which our positive or negative emotions influence our drive towards the learning action. Imagine that I am feeling anxious about solving an equation because I do not believe that I am capable of such a task and my only interest in doing it is to demonstrate to others that I am not falling behind in comparison to my peers. My emotions are negative, but it is insufficient for improving my motivation merely to try to make me feel less anxious by suggesting that to fail on the task would be positive for me, because it would increase my understanding. This tactic is not necessarily going to increase my motivation, because I am only interested in my performance in comparison to my peers and not in actually understanding equations.

The extent to which we believe we can control the outcome of an action and that this action has some value to us clearly influences how we feel about that action. This idea of *control value* was at the heart of a cognitive-motivational model proposed by Pekrun and colleagues (2002). Pekrun's model describes how our emotions influence our cognition and our strategies, as well as our motivation to complete an action. Each of our emotions can be positive or negative, and each can be activating or deactivating. Thus, being positive alone is insufficient for an emotion to increase or decrease our motivation. An emotion needs to be positive *and* *activating* to be effective in increasing motivation.

The goal-orientation component of Pintrich's value component has typically been defined in terms of two broad orientations, although this conceptualization varies (see, for example, Ames, 1992; Boekaerts, 2003; Dweck and Leggett, 1988): an orientation towards increasing competence (mastery orientation), or an orientation towards increasing performance relative to others (performance orientation). Within the performance orientation there is a further differentiation between one approach directed at achieving high performance and another aimed at avoiding low performance – the former being linked to high achievement and learning, whereas the latter has been associated with worse learning outcomes (see, for example, Harackiewicz *et al.*, 1998). Interestingly, our orientation towards a goal affects our social attitudes too. Mastery-oriented learners are demonstrably more likely to be supportive in collaborative interactions with peers and more likely to engage in 'creative risk-taking' (Damon and Phelps, 1989).

The extent to which we adopt an orientation is not fixed and can be manipulated by contextual and dispositional factors. In 2008, some insightful work conducted by Amanda Harris explored the extent to which children's goal orientation was changed by the way in which the task they were asked to complete was described to them (Harris *et al.*, 2008). One group of children was told that the object of their task was to work out the best strategy. They were told that mistakes didn't matter because they would help them to devise the best strategy (mastery instructions). The other group were told that the object of the task was to complete as many successful actions as possible, and that they would get points for each successful action (performance instructions). The children had all been evaluated prior to the study to ensure that they did not have a strong orientation towards either mastery or performance. The results of this work illustrated that the group of children who were given the mastery instructions engaged in significantly more elaborate problem-solving discussions than those children who were given the performance instructions, who displayed lower levels of metacognitive control.

There is, then, a close connection between motivation and metacognition. The two are interwoven, each having a bidirectional impact on the other, and they are closely related to the concept of self-efficacy.

The embodied self and the importance of context

The importance of our embodiment became apparent to me when I was developing a framework that I could use to take context into account when developing, using and analysing technology to support learning. I had been exploring literature from a broad range of subject areas – from architecture to geography – to try to understand what researchers from these different disciplines could provide that would help me to formulate my interpretation of what we mean by the word 'context'.

Research from urban settings and the built environment included much discussion about space, place and our emotional connections with these. Our relationship with our physical environment can delight us or perturb us. We continually build connections between our emotions and our physical and subjective experiences of the world. Technology has made even everyday spaces come alive and made them capable of new forms of interaction (de Kerckhove and Tursi, 2009; Gaved *et al.*, 2018). In addition to this, the integration of network technologies with everyday objects and the proliferation of data have produced both digital and physical manifestations of our environment that are increasingly blended almost seamlessly into what Manovich (2006) has described as a 'phenomenological gestalt'.

The relationship between context and learning has a long history, and there have been many disagreements. There is a substantial body of research that has tried to persuade us that cognition and learning are fundamentally situated within the world (Brown *et al.*, 1989). There has also been a substantial amount of lobbying by scientists who disagree with the proposition that cognition is situated and that learning must likewise be so. Yet it is hard to deny that there is a role for our physical experience in the world in the way that we construct knowledge and understanding, whether we agree wholeheartedly with the proposition of situated cognition and learning or side with its opponents.

My studies of context and learning were influenced particularly by the work of Paul Dourish (2001) from a human–computer interaction (HCI) perspective. Dourish was concerned with the challenges that ubiquitous computing technology had caused those who were concerned with designing interfaces that adhered to the principles of good HCI. He described embodied interaction as a feature not of the technology but of how that technology was used. It was, he proposed, the *source* of intentionality and not the object of it. I drew a connection between the idea of the embodied interaction and the idea of distributed cognition, as described by Hutchins (1995), who talks of ecologies of thinking and studies cognition and learning in everyday settings, such as aircraft cockpits. Interactions with both people and their physical environment are the important connections that create networks of distributed cognition among groups, networks distinct from the cognition of the individuals who make up that group.

Wonderfully detailed work by Chuck Goodwin (2007; 2009) demonstrates the importance of our relationship with our physical environment. He discusses what he refers to as *environmentally coupled gestures* in his analysis of a young learner and her father as they complete some mathematics homework. Goodwin uses his descriptions of the way in which the father combines the language that he uses with the gestures he employs and the structure of the environment. He weaves these together to communicate with his daughter. He pays attention to the position of his body in relation to her, to the different directions of their gaze and to the combined forces of these gestures. Goodwin uses the term *co-operative semiosis* to describe the transformational process through which signs within a context are processed, synthesized and used to create a new context. Meaning and action are built through this social process.

All of these researchers were expanding the boundaries of what they saw as a very narrow perception of human cognition. Dourish's work has much in common with the earlier theories about situated cognition and he uses the term 'coupling' to describe how we make meaning from our moment-by-moment interactions with the world. Meaning-making occurs through our interactions in the world, which vary in their form and structure, through our sharing of meaning with other people and through our relationship with our own thoughts. Dourish referred to these as: ontology, intersubjectivity and intentionality. I wonder, however, if these might also be considered as *proxies for different aspects of intelligence*.

Before leaving this discussion about embodiment, and in particular the importance of context to learning and intelligence, I'd like to note how peculiar I find it that so much published empirical educational research fails to report or even record contextual information. This is particularly strange in light of the fact that there is a huge literature within the social sciences, including education, that demonstrates the impact of context on learning (Luckin, 2010). It is also odd that so little attention is paid to reporting the contextual features of empirical settings in a research area where large trials that would yield generalizable findings are rarely possible. Research transferability relies upon being able to demonstrate the similarity of the two settings across which research transfer is proposed. Therefore, without this contextual information, we reduce the possibilities of research transferability.

This omission within educational research, and educational technology research specifically, became very clear to me in 2012, when I worked with my colleagues Brett Bligh, Andrew Manches, Shaaron Ainsworth, Charles Crook and Richard Noss to conduct a review of the evidence about the effective uses of educational technology (Luckin *et al.*, 2012). We started out with the intention of cataloguing the contextual factors in all of the research evidence that we reviewed. We wanted to record factors within the environment and the resources (both human and inanimate) that were available to participants, and we wanted to understand the nature of the knowledge or skill that the research was exploring and the curriculum, or customs and practice, within which it was situated. We soon discovered that this intention of ours would remain merely that: an intention, because none of the research papers and reports that we reviewed contained anywhere near enough information about these contextual factors to make it worth our while to attempt to develop our catalogue. I was shocked to find that many articles had little information about the who and what and where of the educational intervention that was being proposed, observed or evaluated. It is true that much of the research we reviewed took place in 'real-world' rather than laboratory conditions, and therefore the problem is not that the work is invalid; it is rather that without the contextual data to accompany the results the real value of the research for learners and teachers is undermined. This stark realization made me question the value of most of this research to anyone other than the scientists within the communities of peers who would read the work. How could any of it be applied in the real world without the provision of more information about the setting in which it had been conducted? If, as scientists, we are proud to provide evidence about the importance of context for learning and teaching, then we must also acknowledge this in the research that we are conducting. I will return to this subject in Chapter 6 when I consider the implications for education of the rise in AI technologies.

Perceived self-efficacy

In 1982, Stanford professor Albert Bandura (1982: 201) wrote in the *American Psychologist* journal that 'perceived self-efficacy is concerned with judgements of how well one can execute courses of action required to deal with prospective situations'. In this article, he provided evidence that higher levels of perceived self-efficacy were related to higher levels of performance. He observed that people avoided activities if they believed they were not capable of coping with them, but performed with confidence in those tasks they believed they were capable of coping with – so long as that self-perception was correct. This means that it is extremely important to apprehend our self-efficacy correctly, because inaccuracies can lead to wasted effort and dissatisfaction.

We need strong and accurate judgements about our self-efficacy if we are to put in the effort required to achieve a difficult task and to make accurate decisions about when tasks are too difficult for us to achieve. Bandura believed that the concept of perceived self-efficacy had explanatory power that could account for a wide range of issues including those of relevance to education, such as self-regulation and career choice. He also postulated an influential role for perceived collective self-efficacy in the process of social change.

There is strong evidence that self-efficacy beliefs are related to learning and performance. Believing that one is able to perform a task is strongly related to high performance and learning. The importance of perceived self-efficacy is not limited to students: teachers' perceptions of their own self-efficacy are also important. Teachers' perceptions of self-efficacy have been shown to influence their instructional practices, enthusiasm, commitment and teaching. Positive and accurate perceptions of self-efficacy in teachers have also been related to higher levels of student achievement and student motivation (Skaalvik and Skaalvik, 2007; Woolfolk Hoy and Burke Spero, 2005; Wolters and Daugherty, 2007; Klassen *et al.*, 2009). The notion of self-efficacy is also related to metacognition, and in particular to metacognitive control. Self-efficacy, however, varies depending on the task and environment.

Lee (2009) conducted an interesting study of the OECD Programme for International Student Assessment (PISA) database. He searched the database for the best non-cognitive predictors of achievement in mathematics and identified three student self-belief variables that were significant. These were:

- *self-concept,* defined as learners' perceptions of self, which might be embodied in a statement such as 'I understand even the most difficult work in my mathematics course';
- *self-efficacy,* defined as learners' beliefs about their capability to produce outcomes, which would be reflected in statements such as: 'I am sure I can do difficult work in my mathematics course';
- *anxiety,* defined as learners' physio-emotional reactions when thinking about or performing a task, revealed in statements such as: 'I often worry that it will be difficult for me to do the work in my mathematics course'.

Lee showed that across all OECD countries all three self-belief variables had significant correlations with student achievement scores in mathematics. Self-efficacy, i.e. students' beliefs about their capability to achieve, had the highest positive correlation with student achievement. It was more highly correlated than students' self-concept, which included their beliefs about their understanding, and than students' anxiety.

Perceived self-efficacy combines elements of both metacognition and motivation, and the three concepts are inextricably bound together. I believe that our perceived self-efficacy also draws on our epistemic cognition in important ways. An accurate perceived self-efficacy requires an accurate, evidence-based judgement about our knowledge and understanding. We need to know our ability to succeed in a specific situation and to accomplish tasks both alone and with others for our perceived self-efficacy to be accurate. To make judgements from the evidence about our knowledge and understanding, we need to recognize what good evidence is and we need to know how to make judgements. These facilities relate to our epistemic cognition.

An accurate perceived self-efficacy, based on accurate judgements about what we know, is a key ability for learning, now and in the future. I believe that accurate perceived self-efficacy will be *the* most important ability for our future lifelong learning, because accurate perceived self-efficacy is something that AI cannot replicate. No AI developed to date understands itself; no AI has the human capability for metacognitive awareness, motivation and self-knowledge. We must therefore ensure that we develop our human knowledge and skills to take advantage of what is uniquely human and use AI wisely to do what it does best: the routine cognitive and mechanical skills that we have spent decades instilling in learners and testing in order to award qualifications. The implications of this for school systems, the curriculum and teaching are profound, and educators must engage in discussing what needs to change as a matter of urgency. I will discuss how we might address this need within education in Chapter 5.

Summary

In this third chapter, I have moved on from what it means to know something to the meta-level of human intelligence: our intelligence about ourselves. This self-knowledge, or perhaps I should say self-intelligence, is essential to increasing the sophistication of our knowledge of the world, the way we think about what knowledge is and how we come to know something. As we saw in Chapter 2, we are often unsophisticated in thinking about what knowledge is and how it is gained. The emphasis in this chapter is upon seeing intelligence as more than knowledge about the world, important as this is. I have drawn your attention to the fact that self-knowledge takes us beyond what artificially intelligent systems can achieve.

We increase our ability to construct knowledge and understanding as we interact in the world through our cognitive development. This world-knowledge and understanding is often confused with intelligence, and it is also where artificial intelligence systems excel. However, we do not place sufficient value on our other capabilities that are uniquely human and that complement our knowledge and understanding of the world. We do not value our awareness of our own thinking or our ability to regulate our mental processes. These assets are rarely, if ever, explicitly evaluated in our education systems.

Our meta-intelligence includes four elements:

- *metacognition*: our knowledge and control of our own cognitive processes;
- *meta-emotion*: our awareness of how we feel and how this affects what we know and how we learn;
- *metacontextual awareness*: our physical and mental awareness of the world; and
- *perceived self-efficacy*.

Metacognition can be broken down further into knowing about our knowing – our knowledge of our cognitive processes, about how, when, where and why to know – and the processes that we use to monitor and regulate these cognitive processes. We know that sophisticated metacognition is important for intellectual development and for our performance in school and beyond. We also know that the sophistication of our metacognition can be developed and improved with appropriate teaching and support. There is a plethora of evidence that supports the relationship between metacognition and our intellectual performance: put simply, increasing our metacognitive skills and abilities improves learning outcomes and cognitive performance.

However, even people with highly sophisticated and well-developed metacognition can be starkly unaware of how their knowledge, understanding and beliefs about the world are changed by their experiences with the world. Evidence suggests that our beliefs are coupled to the specific context in which they were formed, and later in our lives we often evaluate our historical beliefs incorrectly; we often do not realize how our beliefs have changed. We also need to acknowledge the connection between metacognition and epistemic cognition. Accurately recalling our past beliefs is more difficult than recalling our current beliefs. To remember what we once believed requires us to reconstruct the results of our mental processing at a previous time, as well as the circumstances of these mental processes. We are not naturally drawn to mental exertion and we are therefore often sucked into our easily-called-upon ability to construct wonderfully convincing post hoc rationalizations of our past thinking and beliefs.

There is a complex dilemma held within our meta-intelligence. It is what sets us apart from artificially intelligent systems, it is the X-factor of our intellectual prowess, and yet it is also home to our human fallibility. This fallibility means that we often do not realize that our beliefs have changed; this leaves us prey to belief manipulation by less scrupulous folk. The case is even more worrying when we combine this human meta-intelligence fallibility with our unsophisticated understanding about how knowledge is justified by evidence. This makes the recent concerns about fake news even more worrying (see, for example, Titcomb and Carson, 2018; Digital, Culture, Media and Sport Committee, n.d.). We clearly need to pay great attention to our meta-intelligence if we want to avoid being duped too often in the future.

The human fallibility dilemma also makes life more complicated for our efforts to talk about evidence in a public context. Should we make people more aware of their vulnerability to belief manipulation? If we do, will they be less open to alternative beliefs and to reading fresh evidence? There are both positive and negative consequences to this more cautious behaviour, and we need an education system that brings out the positive, astute-reasoning benefit, not the closed-mind deficit.

Meta-intelligence is about more than knowing about and regulating our thinking; it is also about knowing and regulating our *feelings* about what we know and how we learn. Evidence from across the social, psychological and neural sciences demonstrates what instinctively we all know: that the way we feel impacts on what and how we learn. Motivation is a particular and an important instance of how our emotions affect our actions, and vice versa. Our emotions drive our actions to increase our knowledge and understanding of the world through our learning.

Our motivation to learn is, as we saw, closely intertwined with our metacognition. Our motivation to learn involves our beliefs about:

- our ability to complete a learning action, including our power to control the outcomes of our actions, and how effectively we believe we are likely to perform;

- the value of the learning action under consideration, which may be influenced by our goal orientation, which in turn can be easily influenced;
- our emotional reactions to any particular learning being proposed to us, bearing in mind that each of our emotions can be positive or negative, and each can be activating or deactivating, and that an emotion needs to be both positive and activating to be effective in increasing motivation.

The penultimate element of our meta-intelligence is concerned with our physical presence in the world and our awareness of it: our *metacontextual intelligence*. There is a substantial amount of evidence that demonstrates how our context impacts upon our learning, from research about the significance of family background to children's learning outcomes, to research about the difficulty people have in transferring what they learn in one context to apply it to a different context. And yet little attention is paid to the contexts in which learning takes place when educational studies are reported. Even less attention is paid to people's knowledge and understanding of their context, and how it changes. Once again, we find the idea of metacontextual intelligence undervalued, and once again this is an intelligence that is not available in any real way to artificially intelligent systems.

The final element in my discussion of meta-intelligence concerns *perceived self-efficacy*. I talked about the evidence indicating that people who have higher levels of perceived self-efficacy perform better. Inaccuracies in our perceived self-efficacy can lead to wasted effort and dissatisfaction. Perceived self-efficacy is important for all of us. It is related to the other elements of meta-intelligence, all of which are inextricably bound together and draw on our epistemic cognition in important ways. An accurate perceived self-efficacy based on accurate judgements about what we know is a key ability for learning, now and in the future. I have expressed the view that accurate perceived self-efficacy will be *the* most important ability for our future lifelong learning, because it is something that is unavailable to AI.

In Chapter 4 we will use the various elements of intelligence that we have discussed in chapters 2 and 3 to explore what artificial intelligence can achieve now, and what it might be able to achieve in the future.

Chapter 4

Talking about intelligence in humans and machines

Intelligence is complex. In chapters 2 and 3 I discussed the elements of intelligence that I believe are important to the way in which we talk about it and evaluate it. Intelligence is about knowing about the world around us and understanding how we come to know about it. It also involves meta-intelligence: our knowledge and regulation of our intelligence. In this chapter I will pull together the different elements of intelligence and meta-intelligence into an interwoven whole: an intelligence we can recognize, support and develop.

The School of Cognitive and Computing Sciences at the University of Sussex, affectionately referred to as COGS, was an amazing place to study computer science and artificial intelligence at the end of the 1990s. It was internationally renowned as a centre of excellence and its interdisciplinary approach gave students an excellent grounding in the fundamentals of intelligence, both artificial and human. One of the most pleasurable aspects of studying at Sussex was being taught by the philosopher Margaret (Maggie) Boden. I had never studied philosophy before I arrived at Sussex, but having Maggie as a tutor and lecturer opened my eyes to the pleasure of thinking in a philosophical way.

All first-year undergraduates in COGS were offered a course in the history of AI, taught by Maggie. I would sit in wonder, enchanted by the narrative that she would weave to teach us fledgling intellectuals about the early history of our human fascination with intelligence. She described the moving mechanical devices called automata (αὐτόματον) that have existed since the earliest centuries. These mechanical marvels were built to imitate human beings or animals, from bears playing drums to ladies playing harpsichords, and some were extremely elaborate. These feats of early engineering were not mere follies: they illustrate our human fascination with building things in our own image, and they are part of the evolutionary story of robotics. We learned that the more cognitively inspired machines evolved in a slightly later period, from the early calculating machines of the 1600s, through the steam-powered mechanical calculators of Charles Babbage (which included the first programmable mechanical calculator, called the analytical engine), to the IBM Mark 1 Computer. These 'cognitive' machines, however, did not attempt to mimic the appearance of humans; they merely aimed to emulate our capacity to calculate.

The word 'robot' was introduced in the 1920s by the Czech writer Karel Čapek (Wikipedia, n.d.c.), who used it to describe a race of artificial humans in a future dystopia. Robots of all sorts have been the fodder of novelists and filmmakers since this time, mainly for dystopian future scenario painting. The more serious side of the study of robotics emanated from the work of Norbert Wiener (1950), who started the field of cybernetics in the 1940s in order to study animal control and communication so as to build machines that could copy these functions effectively.

I use the word *robot* in this book to encompass all of the different manifestations of work that is being done to create machines that can emulate human intelligent behaviour. The term artificial intelligence, or AI, has been somewhat restricted in recent years to a focus on machine learning. Machine learning is just a particular approach to developing artificially intelligent technology, although it must be said that machine learning is also an extremely useful approach to AI. However, to understand the real implications of AI and our relationship to it, we need to consider a broader definition for AI.

The *Oxford Dictionary of English* (2005) defines AI as

> computer systems that have been designed to interact with the world through capabilities (for example, visual perception and speech recognition) and intelligent behaviours (for example, assessing the available information and then taking the most sensible action to achieve a stated goal) that we would think of as essentially human ('AI', 2005).

More recently, AI has been defined as the domain of computer systems capable of actions and behaviours 'that require intelligence when done by humans' (Copeland, 2000). This ties any evaluation of AI to a comparison with human intelligence. An older definition of AI, which has been immensely useful for many decades, can be found in Alan Turing's groundbreaking work. In his 1950 paper 'Computing machinery and intelligence', he stated 'I believe that at the end of the century the use of words and general educated opinion will have altered so much that one will be able to speak of machines thinking without expecting to be contradicted' (Turing, 1950). Turing also devised a test called the 'Imitation Game', in which an interrogator was charged with differentiating between a man and a woman, whom he could not see, by asking them questions – Turing asks whether if a machine took the place of the man the interrogator would be more or less able to differentiate the woman. Once again, Turing's test here tied any evaluation of the intelligence of technology to a comparison with human intelligence. It is also an interesting definition, because of its focus on deception.

At the start of this book I highlighted my concern that our obsession with measuring and simplicity was robbing us of our ability to make good judgements and causing us to value things inappropriately. I suggest that there are many technologies that can deceive their users into believing they are human. However, I would suggest that this is more a reflection of our propensity to undervalue what it means to be human than a real reflection of the intelligence of the technologies.

As well as defining AI we also need to differentiate between the terms *domain-specific* (or *narrow*) *intelligence*, as claimed for some AI systems such as IBM's Watson and Deepmind's AlphaGo, and *artificial general intelligence* (AGI). Domain-specific intelligence requires that behaviour is intelligent within a very fixed boundary, such as playing a game like chess or go, driving a vehicle, or storing, retrieving and applying information to specific questions. AGI describes the point at which an AI-powered computer or robot becomes capable of redesigning and improving itself or of designing AI more advanced than itself. This type of AI would have to successfully perform *any* intellectual task that a human being could. This capacity for general intelligence is translated in AI terms into the phrase *the singularity*.

In his highly influential book *Life 3.0: Being human in the age of artificial intelligence*, Max Tegmark (2017) was also keen to find a definition for AI that did not rely on a direct comparison to human intelligence capability. He wanted a generally applicable definition that was broad and that would be useful now and in the future. He defined today's artificial intelligence systems as being only narrowly intelligent because, while they were able to accomplish complex goals, each AI system was only able to accomplish goals that were very specific. His emphasis on the accomplishment of complex goals arises from his definition of intelligence, which is the 'ability to accomplish complex goals [that] can't be measured by a single IQ, only by an ability spectrum across all goals' (Tegmark, 2017: 51). He added that general intelligence included the ability to learn. Interestingly, however, his definition of AGI reverts again to a comparison with human intelligence and defines AGI as the 'ability to accomplish any cognitive task at least as well as humans' (ibid., 39).

I like the idea of coupling intelligence with learning and the accomplishment of complex goals. However, I am less keen on the use of purely cognitive tasks in any judgement about human intelligence. I will return to the subject of human intelligence shortly, because that is the main focus of this book. But for now it is the question of robot intelligence that concerns me. And I include within the term *robot* any sort of technology-based intelligence, whether purely software or embodied as a robot.

Tegmark's definition of narrowly intelligent AI explains the limitations of this intelligence very well: it is confined to very specific applications. It is fairly clear that these AI systems may be able to outwit even the smartest of human systems at the very specific skill they have been trained to achieve, such as playing a complex game or searching for a specific clause among millions of documents. However, these AI systems are extremely constrained, not just to the specific task for which they have been trained, but also by the types of task for which their skills are appropriate. These systems are not intelligent like humans, and we should stop considering that they are anything other than extremely fast information processing systems that can complete a specific function reliably and accurately. They are not yet in the same league as human intelligence, and we should stop talking about them in human terms. Nevertheless, they will transform our lives and we need to increase our human intelligence in order to make sure that this transformation is a positive one.

What is human intelligence?

I return now to the main focus of this book, which is about how the methods we use for identifying, talking about and valuing human intelligence are impoverished. As a consequence of these impoverished tools we are at risk of dumbing down rather than enhancing the most valuable resource in the world: ourselves.

The way in which we identify, evaluate and talk about human intelligence must encompass all of the elements that I discussed in chapters 2 and 3. In particular, it must encompass the 'rational' subsystem of our System 2 that will drive us to be the self-effective learners we need to be in order to outwit any AI. I stress here the importance of learning because, in accordance with Max Tegmark, I believe that learning is fundamental to intelligence, something we must improve at and something that we must undertake throughout our lives. It is an intelligence that is also fallible, prone to bias and amazingly good at post hoc rationalization in order to maintain self-esteem.

I have already suggested that it is time for us to make a paradigm shift in the way we think and talk about human intelligence. We therefore need to engage in more than linear progress towards a slightly revised conceptualization of intelligence. We need to engage our subjective experiences as scientists in order to move beyond the boundaries of our current conceptualization. So, how might a human intelligence be better framed? I unpacked the different human capabilities that I consider to be essential to human intelligence in chapters 2 and 3. I now present these as the seven elements of an interwoven intelligence model that I suggest is more useful for developing our human intelligence and staying ahead of our AI.

Interwoven intelligence

I propose that there are seven elements to human level intelligence. Five of these elements can be considered under the heading *meta-intelligence*. I use the word *element* because it characterizes something that is essential and significant. Each element in this interwoven intelligence model comes without any expectation that it be a particular size or shape, or manifest fixed dimensions. Throughout our lives we develop our intelligence within and across the seven elements that I propose, some more quickly than others. I must stress that these are not separate intelligences, but different elements of a complex, interwoven whole. Not only are the individual elements differentially sophisticated at any moment in time, but the relationships between them are complex and varied. For example, a highly sophisticated knowledge about physics or history may not be matched by an evenly sophisticated social intelligence.

To be intelligent we need to develop sophistication across all seven elements. However, while all of the elements are important, both in themselves and through their relationships with other elements, some elements may be more important for some people than others, or at some times in our lives in comparison to other times. Our development within and across these elements is complementary and no element can be ignored: all are essential, but naturally sometimes we may excel in our development of some elements as compared to others. The precise nature of the composition of our individual interwoven intelligence will be as individual as our fingerprints, but unlike our fingerprints we can develop and enrich our interwoven intelligence throughout our lives: it is not fixed at birth. The secret to success in the development of interwoven intelligence is to ensure that we approach it holistically and that we avoid focusing on any individual component alone, or on any subgroup: we must focus on all seven.

Table 4.1: Interwoven intelligence: academic, social and meta-intelligence

	Element name	Element description
1	Academic intelligence	*Knowledge about the world.* Knowledge and understanding that is multi and interdisciplinary. Knowledge is not the same as information, but we frequently muddle them up. We need to stop doing this.
2	Social intelligence	*Social interaction capabilities.* Social interaction is the basis of individual thought and of communal intelligence. AI cannot achieve human-level social interaction. There is also a meta-aspect to social intelligence, through which we can develop an awareness of and the ability to regulate our own social interactions.

Meta-intelligence

	Element name	Element description
3	Meta-knowing intelligence	*Knowing about knowledge.* Epistemic intelligence, or our personal epistemology. We must develop an understanding of what knowledge is, what it means to know something, what good evidence is and how to make judgements based on that evidence and our context.
4	Metacognitive intelligence	*Includes regulation skills.* We need to learn and develop the ability to interpret our own ongoing mental activity, and these interpretations need to be grounded in good evidence about our contextualized interactions in the world.
5	Metasubjective intelligence	*Metasubjective knowledge, and skilled metasubjective regulation.* The term *metasubjective* encompasses both our emotional and motivational knowledge and regulatory skills. We need to develop our ability to recognize our emotions and the emotions of others, to regulate our emotions and behaviours with respect to other people and with respect to taking part in a particular activity (our motivation).

	Element name	Element description
6	Metacontextual intelligence	Metacontextual knowledge and skills are essential for understanding the way in which our physical embodiment interacts with our environment, its resources and with other people. Metacontextual intelligence includes physical intelligence, through which we use our bodies to interact with and learn about the world. Metacontextual intelligence is our intellectual bridge to our instinctive mental processes; it allows us to recognize when they are demanding attention and evaluate whether that attention is warranted. Metacontextual intelligence will also help us to recognize when we are biased and when we are succumbing to post hoc rationalization.
7	Perceived self-efficacy	This intelligence element requires an *accurate, evidence-based judgement about our knowledge and understanding, our emotions and motivations and our personal context.* We need to know our ability to succeed in a specific situation and to accomplish tasks both alone and with others. This is the most important element of human intelligence and it is highly connected to the other six elements.

My motivation for introducing these seven elements is not an obsession with categorization, and it is certainly not a fascination with measurement. I will, however, consider the question of evaluation and measurement in Chapter 6 when I discuss the implications of thinking about intelligence in this way. Instead, I am motivated by finding a way to value human intelligence that can be useful in helping us to develop our intelligence continually. These elements are therefore essentially developmental and there is no finished intelligence state that each of us should aim to achieve before we die; it is rather that these elements can act as guides as we work to develop the sophistication of our human intelligence constantly. I am not suggesting that this is a complete picture of human intelligence, but I do believe that it is a useful way to think and talk about intelligence as we work out the best way to outwit the robots.

Together, the seven elements of intelligence outlined here form an interwoven whole, the complexity of which cannot be described in terms of dimensions or shapes. I am sure my colleagues in mathematics or chemistry will be able to come up with the right words to describe the way in which the seven elements of intelligence are connected. However, in their absence I have settled for the word *interwoven* and therefore describe my model of human intelligence as being one of *interwoven intelligence*.

My selection and description of each of the seven elements included within this interwoven intelligence is grounded in a sound and significant body of evidence. It is evidence that demonstrates that each of these elements has been established to have an important and consequential relationship to our intelligent performance in the world. I'll emphasize again, lest there be any confusion: *these are not seven separate intelligences.* Yes, some of us may have greater sophistication in one element and lesser sophistication in another; we may have more sophisticated metacognitive awareness of our knowledge and understanding of physics than we do of our knowledge and understanding of music, but neither our physics, our music nor our metacognitive awareness of them is a separate intelligence.

The developmental nature of interwoven intelligence reflects that we all develop the form and sophistication of these seven intelligence elements at different rates and times and to different extents. This development is not linear or even across all elements and we will all develop at different rates. Our abilities within and across each of these seven elements are inconsistent across different subject areas, and across different environmental and social settings. It is also highly likely that there will be incoherent aspects within these elements, because as humans we know that we can hold seemingly contradictory beliefs about things at the same time. It is not unintelligent to hold such beliefs. However, a measure of our intelligence would need to encompass the extent to which we are aware of these incoherent beliefs, and it would need to encompass recognition of the way in which we learn from these incoherencies and aim to achieve greater stability.

We might want to modify our evaluation to take into account the fact that a human baby will not be able to demonstrate any of these elements yet, but that we believe he or she has the capability to demonstrate these elements. We therefore believe he or she also has the capability to be intelligent through growth, social interaction, experience and development.

I use the word *sophisticated* to describe the quality that each element of our intelligence needs to become, bearing in mind of course that greater sophistication will always be possible, no matter how sophisticated our intelligence becomes. We don't start with intelligence of a sophisticated quality; we must develop this sophistication, and we will therefore naturally pass through different phases of sophistication. However, within any of the elements it will always be possible for us to attain a sophisticated level for certain applications of that intelligence element while not attaining the same quality of sophistication for other applications of the same intelligence element. For example, I may be skilled at regulating my emotional and motivational state with respect to my physical fitness, but not with respect to my mathematics homework.

In addition to the term sophisticated, I suggest that we describe lower levels of sophistication in each of the seven intelligence elements using the following descriptors based on previous research in the areas of epistemic and metacognitive knowledge and skills: *simple, complex* and *integrated*. The way we describe each of these levels will be different for each of the seven elements of intelligence. I will address the detail of these descriptions in Chapter 6 when I discuss assessment.

So, are robots intelligent?

I dealt rather cursorily with this question with respect to narrow AI earlier, because it is relatively straightforward to conclude that while the achievements of the best of modern AI are extremely impressive, such AI is, nevertheless, very limited in its intelligence. But are there more sophisticated forms of AI that we should take into consideration before we leave this question? In order to address the intelligence of these more sophisticated forms of AI, I'll provide a very brief description of current trends in AI technologies.

In general AI can seem like magic until we understand how it works, and there is a fair amount of terminology that just adds to the sense of magic. We therefore need to bust some terminology before we actually address the question of AI sophistication in the future.

AI that cannot learn

All AI is based in digital technology that is capable of computation. It is worth noting for the sake of completeness that it is possible for AI to be connected to a biological system, or to operate within a biological system, but at least some of the AI remains digitally based. A prerequisite for computation is the ability to store information. This storage in digital technology takes the form of a 1 or 0, on your computer's hard disk for example. The computation completed by the technology is simply a case of taking information that has been stored in this way and transforming it through processing it so that it becomes different information. This processing of digital information is done by means of a pre-defined function. The instructions that define the functions that transform information from one state to another take the form of algorithms. These algorithms can be written in many different languages according to the type of computation that is desired. The instructions in an algorithm can lead to extremely complex computations, particularly when AI is involved.

This model of computation is the basis of all computers, including those that implement AI. The difference in the various types of AI is mainly to be found in the way that the instructions of the algorithms are written, and the way that the information that is to be transformed by those instructions is structured. The algorithms at the heart of many of the early AI systems used rules, in what were called production rule-based or knowledge-based systems. These systems were able to complete search, planning, decision-making and game playing. These systems operated via a series of logical IF-THEN rules. The information that was given to the AI system through the keyboard of the computer was mapped to a matching IF statement in one of the rules. When this mapping occurred, the rule would be implemented. For example, a rule of the form IF the input is 'yellow' THEN output 'colour of the sun'. This is obviously a very simple example, but remarkably complex systems can be built using this IF-THEN rule technique. The rule base could be complex and interlinked to allow these systems to solve complex problems.

In my first year as an undergraduate AI student I was asked to write an AI computer program that implemented a version of one of the first AI systems. The original system was the 'brainchild' of Joseph Weizenbaum. It was developed in 1964 and it was called ELIZA. This early AI program was designed to show the superficiality of communication between people and machines, although many people attributed human-like feelings to ELIZA. ELIZA mimicked a psychoanalyst and invited its users to type their problems into a text-based interface. For example, I might type: 'I am really worried that someone is following me'. And the computer screen response from ELIZA might be something like: 'Why do you think that someone is following you?'

Within the ELIZA program a process of pattern matching would have occurred, and when words in the phrase I had typed were matched to a rule in the ELIZA rule base then that rule would have been processed to produce the resulting response. The words 'I am really worried that' from my input phrase could be matched to a rule of the form: 'IF I xx worried that $xxxxx$ THEN Why are you xx worried that $xxxxx$'.

For my undergraduate assignment, I decided to implement a politician ELIZA who would parrot back a version of whatever input phrase was entered, and if no rules fired there was a default rule that brought a 'change of subject' response from the politician ELIZA. This worked very well because the sort of conversation that might take place with a politician is fairly predictable, in the same way as the conversations between patients and psychoanalysts.

For example, I might type: 'What are you going to do about your record on the economy, which is taking a turn for the worse?' And the computer screen response from my politician ELIZA might be something like: 'We are going to keep to our manifesto promises about the economy, which is taking a turn for the better'. I might then type: 'But unemployment is going up and economic growth is going down, how will you address this?' And the computer screen response from my politician ELIZA might be something like: 'We shall continue to implement our sound economic policy to increase growth and reduce unemployment'. I might then type: 'But why do you think these policies will work now, when they have not worked for the past three years?' And the computer screen response from my politician ELIZA might be something like: 'It is important we remember the positive achievements and this government's impeccable track record'. And so on ...

However, despite the fact that many people were impressed by early systems such as ELIZA, the challenges of representing knowledge using rules were considerable and the systems were very limited in what they could do. For example, it was not precisely clear how many rules were needed for a particular scenario, and it was hard to know what an adequate number of rules might be. It was also hard to know what should happen in special cases and to know how rules could be designed to be consistent as well as sufficient. In short, to be successful, it was essential that these systems had the right features to represent the problem they were supposed to be solving. They also needed sufficient, consistent knowledge and the ability to deal with exceptions, because in the real world there are almost always exceptions. In addition, these early systems were very limited because their rule bases were fixed at the time of their design, and they had no capability to learn. The real transformation in the fortunes of AI technology came with the development of algorithms that produced systems that could learn.

AI that can learn

There are various ways in which AI systems can be programmed to be able to learn beyond the fixed set of instructions written at the time of their design. One way of achieving learning is through a set of probability-based rules about the environment in which the system is operating. The probability parameters in these rules can be changed as the machine learns. The system must find the right rules to match the observed data. Statistical learning algorithms have been used for voice recognition, for example (see for more detail Hinton and Salakhutdinov, 2006; Hinton *et al.*, 2012), and they assume large amounts of data from which the likelihood of something happening in the environment can be calculated as a percentage. A set of prior probabilities is used to bootstrap the process; the system can then be trained using the available datasets. The extent of the learning is a factor of the quality of the training data and the subsequent data encountered by the system. The system is limited by the rules that describe the 'world' of problems that it can tackle. Put another way, these systems can only work with a finite collection of input types.

Neural networks, a manifestation of this kind of learning AI system, are not new. I remember learning about them as an undergraduate and building programs using neural networks as a way of developing AI that could learn. However, their popularity has increased over the last decade, as has their sophistication. Neural networks are so named because they are inspired by the structure of our brains' neurons. They are, however, very different from the human brain in nature. The original neural net theory was developed in the middle of the last century through what was called the McCulloch Pitts (MP) analysis (McCulloch and Pitts, 1943). This was a logical, rule-based system that was likened to the firing of a neuron. An artificial MP neuron was basically a logic gate: it was described as 'firing' when it was given an input statement that was true. When the MP neuron did not fire, the input statement was deemed false. Different MP neurons could have different firing thresholds, such that an MP neuron with a high threshold value was inhibitory and would rarely fire. This was a representation of a logical 'and'. An MP neuron with a low threshold value represented a logical 'or'.

These MP neurons were the building blocks of the logic systems in early neural networks. Any logical expression could be represented by a network of these MP neurons. However, these systems were restricted by the sorts of inputs they could process. This limitation stimulated the use of the concept of *functions*, a type of machine with inputs that are a collection of numerical measurements that then generate a set of outputs, which are also represented as a pattern of numbers. This sort of situation is quite common in areas such as speech and image processing, or problem-solving involving the control of physical devices and systems.

The MP neurons were used by a psychologist called Frank Rosenblatt to build a system called a Perceptron (Rosenblatt, 1957). The Perceptron had three layers of MP neurons. The first layer of the Perceptron accepted the input information and the third layer acted as output units. Between the two layers was a middle layer of 'association' neurons that were also called 'hidden' units. The connections from the input units to the hidden units were randomly fixed (modelling some particular disposition) and not modifiable, while the connections from the hidden units to the output units were modifiable and changed their values depending upon the Perceptron's training. Rosenblatt's 'Perceptron learning theorem' meant that the system could 'remember' what it had been trained with, but it was not always able to deal with inputs on which it had not been trained.

The Perceptron work was done in the late 1950s, but it has influenced today's deep learning methods, which aim to learn a useful set of features representing the learning machine's environment. Deep learning methods tend to focus on learning machines that have multiple layers of processing units or neural networks. So, for example, the inputs to the system are processed by input units. The features for the input units are chosen by the artificial intelligence engineer. Then the outputs of the input units are fed into the inputs of the first layer of hidden units, and the outputs of this first layer of hidden units are fed into the inputs of a second layer of hidden units. This process continues until the final layer of hidden units is reached. At this point the output of the final layer of hidden units is used to make a prediction: to give an answer. This describes the process of supervised machine learning.

Processing through a series of nodes in a neural network may not sound as if it should lead to the solution of complex problems, but these deep learning networks can achieve some impressive feats. In fact, these deep neural networks can lead to results that even the developers had not expected. These neural networks are 'black box' machines that cannot explain the decisions they make or the actions they take. And this lack of transparency is a considerable problem, one that limits the usefulness of these smart technologies – and one to which AI companies are now paying increasing attention.

My briefest of brief summaries of AI technologies above is provided with the purpose of highlighting the fact that all AI systems are based on a core set of technology approaches. The higher-level discussions about an AI that should dominate the design process before any particular technology is selected are the discussions about the particular problem the AI is to solve. This might, for example, be to diagnose a cancerous tumour, or to recognize that the person standing in front of the AI is the same person as the photograph in the passport being presented to the AI.

If we take away the physical manifestation of AI in robots, androids or whatever, and think about the essence of AI and how it is done, then the most important aspect of AI is the design process, through which a clear specification of the problem to be solved by the AI is developed. From this a clear *problem specification* and a proposed solution can be developed. Without these problem (and solution) specifications, there is no possibility of developing an AI that will effectively meet the aims of its developers. How knowledge is represented and how information is represented for an AI to process will determine whether or not a particular problem is solved.

The situation is not fundamentally different when it is an AI that is developing another AI. At some point in the development of an AI the problem that is to be addressed by the new AI has to be sufficiently specified. Within boundaries there are already AI technologies that can write AI programs, and we already use our AI technologies to help us design AI systems – see, for example, Google AutoML (Google, n.d.). However, the limitations on AI self-reproduction are significant and sophisticated. Human-level, self-reproducing AIs are not imminent.

So, are robots intelligent?

I have proposed a different way of talking about human intelligence and I have discussed the basics of AI, including differentiating between domain-specific intelligence and general intelligence. I have established that narrow, *domain-specific AI systems* – the type of system that is currently proliferating extremely quickly – *are not really intelligent*. It has to be acknowledged that it is possible to build an AI system that can get a high score in an IQ test (*MIT Technology Review*, 2015). However, that IQ test is really a subject-specific test, the subject of study being the completion of an IQ test. The inadequacy of the IQ-test approach to evaluating human intelligence has already been discussed. IQ tests focus only on a very particular way of making judgements about intelligence, a way that does not take into account the rich texture and variety of human intelligence that are essential for human progress in and beyond the 21st century. IQ tests have a narrow focus, just like most AI.

Why might we consider AI systems to be intelligent?

No one who is developing domain-specific AI systems is suggesting that these emulate the intelligence of a human in a holistic sense. The claim is more that each example of domain-specific AI is merely a manifestation of intelligence with particular respect to a constrained domain: a particular environment or problem set. Some people might also claim that each successful implementation of domain-specific AI takes us closer to general AI and the singularity. I am therefore willing to look at each example of domain-specific AI as an example that should be judged against human intelligence only with respect to the particular constrained domain in which the intelligence is being applied. This makes more sense in light of the kinds of media-friendly experiment that pitch human experts against an AI, for example, at the games of Jeopardy, chess or Go. However, even within this more specific test, we are only judging intelligence in terms of the first element of interwoven intelligence – and that is such a diminished way of conceiving of intelligence that I would argue it is not intelligence at all.

A great deal of the reason we are so willing to call something intelligent when it can merely reproduce a slice of the human intelligence pie is because, for decades, we have focused too much on the cognitive aspects of intelligence – Element 1 in the interwoven intelligence model – and too little on the other six aspects of our human intelligence. I am not alone in feeling that the AI systems currently driving innovation are lacking intelligence in some significant ways. One of the catalysts for my concern about the way we are treating AI systems as intelligent stems from my focus on the way AI affects education. Put simply, as a parent and grandparent, I know that I would not trust any teacher (AI or human) who could not explain to me the reasons why they had made a particular decision about my child or grandchild. Current AI systems are not able to explain their decisions, and they have no metacognitive awareness. This is a serious problem for developers who believe that their technology can replace a human teacher. It is also a problem beyond education, as we increasingly probe for our AI systems to explain how they have reached a particular decision.

Machine learning systems are increasingly causing concern to their designers, who do not understand why their system has behaved in a particular way, for example by interpreting people's faces and discerning their sexuality in ways that we do not understand (see, for example, Kuang, 2017). Are these systems making decisions in different ways to human decision-making processes? Could we learn something from the way these machines make decisions? Or are these AIs simply not operating in a manner that is contextualized beyond the constraints of their domain-specific world? Interwoven intelligence elements 5 and 6 require us to know and understand our context and our subjective experience of it, because these factors will impact on the way that we make decisions, even in a domain-specific problem area. Machine learning systems have no access to the contextual and subjective data that we use, and therefore their decisions will of course be reached differently.

A new research programme called Explainable Artificial Intelligence (XAI, also known sometimes as AIX) has been funded by the Defense

Advanced Research Projects Agency (DARPA) in the USA (Gunning, n.d.). This programme will fund research designed to make machine learning able to explain itself. One of the problems highlighted for this program is that of building machine learning systems that can justify their decisions. The DARPA initiative is particularly timely in view of the European Union's General Data Protection Regulation, effective since May 2018, Article 22 of which specifies the right to explanation and means that EU citizens can contest 'legal or similarly significant' decisions made by algorithms and appeal for human intervention.

The second element in the interwoven intelligence model is *personal epistemology*. In Chapter 2, I discussed the research that has sought to characterize epistemic cognition, or personal epistemology, and how it develops, making clear the complexity of thought required for sophisticated epistemic cognition. We need to appreciate that knowledge is something we construct for ourselves, that it is relative to context, that it evolves and is always tentative. How will machine learning algorithms develop the epistemic cognition that is essential to the process of justifying a decision?

Our underestimation of human intelligence has led us down something of a rabbit hole. We have built machines that are incredibly useful and sophisticated. We have, however, made the mistake of calling these machines intelligent, and the mistake of considering them as emulating humans in this respect. We now find ourselves demanding that these poor dumb systems justify and explain their decisions, which is something they were never designed to do. We have failed to realize that all seven elements of the interwoven intelligence model are required for us humans to make valid, defendable decisions.

Hope for the future

Yes, intelligence is complex and it is more than knowledge of the world. However, we can find ways to talk about it that make the limitations of artificially intelligent systems perfectly clear and also reveal the limitations of how we are currently developing our human intelligence in many parts of the world.

The promise of AI is amazing: it will change our world forever, and each of our lives will be subject to the ways in which AI is built and developed by companies that we know very little about. Narrow, domain-specific AI will help us to achieve amazing feats in medicine, science, farming and many other areas. Artificial general intelligence (AGI) or the singularity – the point at which an AI can do everything we humans can, including being capable of redesigning and improving itself or of designing

AI more advanced than itself – is still a long way off. More contemporary concerns are those that relate to the development of an AI that can explain its decisions.

Summary

The interwoven intelligence model presented in this chapter provides a way to talk about the complexity of intelligence and to appreciate how much of it is still beyond any AI. To be intelligent, we need to develop sophistication across all seven elements of the interwoven intelligence model. In short, we need to (1) know about the world, (2) know about what knowledge is, (3) know how to interact socially, and know about (4) our cognition and knowledge, (5) our context, (6) our emotions and (7) our self-efficacy.

Together the seven elements of intelligence outlined here form an interwoven whole, the complexity of which cannot be described in terms of dimensions or shapes. Each of the seven elements is grounded in a sound and significant body of evidence. The developmental nature of interwoven intelligence reflects that we all develop the form and sophistication of these seven intelligence elements at different rates, times and to different extents. Our abilities within and across each of these seven elements is inconsistent across different subject areas, and across different environmental and social settings.

Science must always reach for the stars and strive to achieve the impossible. AI is no exception to this rule. We must therefore explore the realms of XAI ('Explainable AI'; see Gunning, n.d.), and continue to develop our understanding of what it means to be intelligent. However, we also need to appreciate the enormity of this task and must realign our expectations about who or what we should entrust with making important decisions for our future, and on what evidence these decisions are to be based. In Chapter 6, which considers the implications of AI for education systems, I will highlight the need for us to develop in everyone a much greater understanding of data and evidence – how we collect it, analyse it and learn from it, and how we use it effectively to make decisions.

In Chapter 5, we will consider the implications of developments in artificial intelligence and their impact on our relationship to our human intelligence. I will suggest that we need to attend to our human intelligence constantly, and that it is something to be developed and nurtured throughout our lives.

Who moved my intelligence?

In the summer of 2017 I was lucky enough to spend a month working at the University of Sydney. During this stay, I enjoyed watching a television programme from the Australian Broadcasting Commission (ABC) called *The AI Race* (ABC, 2018). The show presented data from a study into the risks to Australian jobs from AI-powered automation (AlphaBeta, 2017). I was relieved for myself to see that according to this data professors are only likely to have 13 per cent of their job automated, while carpenters are predicted to have 55 per cent of what they do performed by smart technology. The ABC reporter explored various jobs and met up with employees to hear their views. For example, Frank, a truck driver, was not persuaded that autonomous trucks would be able to replace his experience and intuition about the behaviour of other humans, whether pedestrian or driver. The autonomous vehicles would not be able to help out other drivers stranded on the roadside or provide customer service on delivery of a load either. He was definitely not convinced that AI was going to replace him any time soon.

Further jobs were explored: the legal profession, for example, where law students were stunned by an AI paralegal that could search through thousands of documents to find a requested clause in a specific document, in no time at all. The law students berated their education for not preparing them for a world of automation. On the one hand we have Frank, who does not believe that AI can replace him, and on the other we have a group of law students who are persuaded that AI can already do a lot of what they are studying to be able to do. Nobody seemed very curious about how they might better prepare themselves for AI's onslaught on their workplace.

I therefore started to consider how I might persuade people that they need to improve their human intelligence constantly in order to prepare themselves for a workplace augmented with AI technology. The key to future success is likely to depend upon our ability to develop the expertise that AI cannot achieve: the unique human intelligence qualities that will be at a premium. In Chapter 4, I suggested a possible way of thinking about intelligence that would help us to recognize more aspects of our human intelligence. We also need education and training designed to ensure that people gain the knowledgeable understanding and skills that will enable them to work effectively with AI and also develop their intelligence in a way that sets them apart from their AI colleagues. I tackle the implications of AI for education in Chapter 6, but in this chapter I focus on how we can use AI to help us develop our own human intelligence.

Who moved my intelligence?

A self-help book might be a good way to communicate to large numbers of people that they need to develop a healthy curiosity about the state of their intelligence and its fitness for purpose in a fast-moving, AI-augmented world. In my search for a successful self-help book on which to think about how an AI self-help book might be framed, I stumbled across *Who Moved My Cheese? An amazing way to deal with change in your work and in your life* (Johnson, 1998).

The book was a story featuring four characters: two mice, called Sniff and Scurry, and two little people, called Hem and Haw. These characters lived together in a maze through which they all searched for cheese (that is, for happiness and success). Their search bore fruit when all of them found cheese in Cheese Station C. Hem and Haw were content with this state of affairs and worked out a schedule for how much cheese they could eat each day. They enjoyed their cheese and relaxed at Cheese Station C. Sniff and Scurry, meanwhile, remained vigilant and kept their wits about them. When – horror of horrors – there was no cheese at Cheese Station C one day, Sniff and Scurry were not surprised: they had seen this coming as the cheese supply had been diminishing. They had prepared themselves for the inevitable arduous cheese-hunt through the maze, and they had already started the new search together and soon found a new cheese supply at Cheese Station N. In contrast Hem and Haw were angry and annoyed when they found the cheese gone. Hem asked: 'Who moved my cheese?' Hem and Haw got angrier, and felt the situation they found themselves in was unfair. Hem was unwilling to search for more cheese and wallowed in feeling victimised; Haw was willing to search but lacked confidence in his ability and took a while to pluck up the courage to search for a fresh supply of cheese.

Haw started his trek into the maze and, while he was still worried, found some scraps of cheese that kept him going as he searched. One day Haw found Cheese Station N, with all its lovely cheese. He reflected on his experience and decided to use the largest wall in the maze to write the following seven messages in the hopes that Hem might one day also search for fresh cheese.

Who moved my cheese?

1. Change Happens: *They Keep Moving the Cheese*
2. Anticipate Change: *Get Ready for the Cheese to Move*
3. Monitor Change: *Smell the Cheese Often So You Know When It Is Getting Old*
4. Adapt to Change Quickly: *The Quicker You Let Go of Old Cheese, The Sooner You Can Enjoy New Cheese*
5. Change: *Move with The Cheese*
6. Enjoy Change! *Savor the Adventure and Enjoy the Taste of New Cheese!*
7. Be Ready to Change Quickly and Enjoy It Again: *They Keep Moving the Cheese* (Johnson, 1998).

While this may seem like an over-engineered metaphor for energizing people to embrace change, the book was in fact extremely popular back in the 1990s. It was also the subject of considerable criticism: that it was too positive about change; that it was patronizing and compared people inappropriately to rats in a maze. Whether we are too positive or too negative about change, whether you are a Frank or a group of law students, it is hard to deny that change will happen. Therefore, I think there is still value in Haw's writing on the wall, so to speak, and I have therefore tried to clarify this value for our current AI dilemma by revising the seven messages written on the cheese maze wall as follows.

Who moved my intelligence?

1. Change happens: *They keep making smarter, more powerful computers*
2. Anticipate change: *Get ready for ever more powerful AI systems*
3. Monitor change: *Keep checking on your own intelligence to make sure you are keeping it fresh*
4. Adapt to change thoughtfully: *The more carefully you offload human intelligence to AI, the more AI can help you educate for sophisticated human intelligence*
5. Change: *Move with the new potential for diversifying human intelligence*
6. Enjoy change! *Savour the journey and enjoy new ways to develop sophisticated human intelligence among more students*
7. Be ready to change and enjoy developing human intelligence again: *They keep making smarter, more powerful computers*

AI *can help humans to move our intelligence*

There is a beautiful irony in our current dilemma. This irony is more than a quirk of fate: it is something that we have created for ourselves, and yet we fail to recognize its beauty. We have created AI technology that can perform tasks some people consider to be part of our intelligence repertoire. We have modelled this AI technology on a diminished understanding of our own human intelligence. And here is the elegant finesse: it is precisely because of the way that we have designed our AI technology that we can now use it to help us develop our human intelligence beyond the ways in which our AI technology can develop its own intelligence – and in ways that will enable us to outwit our AI technology. What do I mean by this?

Let's start with what AI is good at. AI technology is good at processing large amounts of data and looking for patterns in this data. These might be patterns that enable the technology to recognize a particular human face, to find a particular line of text in millions of documents, or to work out the best combination of treatments to match the profile of a particular disease. This processing of large amounts of data with a consistent and unwavering level of performance, and which is not affected by lack of food, lack of sleep or poor health, is beyond our human capabilities. However, now that we are swimming in a sea of data that can capture our every word, movement and action, we can also use our AI technology to process this data, look for patterns in it that represent the development of our human intelligent repertoire, and tell us more about ourselves and our intellect.

MindFit: AI as a 'Fitbit for the mind'

Colleagues such as Judy Kay in Sydney are developing what they call interfaces to Personal Analytics for Learners (iPALs) and interfaces to Personal Analytics for Teachers (iPATs). The object of such activity is to find a good way to engage people in interacting with their personal data and its analysis in a manner that will help their personal intellectual development, either as students or educators. This enterprise can be likened to the development of devices that help people track their physical fitness; iPALs and iPATs might therefore be considered as a sort of somewhat simplified 'Fitbit for the mind'. If we speculate about the kinds of data that we could collect about our intellectual and social interactions, the kinds of data that would help us to track and understand our intellectual well-being as well as our physical fitness and our mental health, could we develop something like a 'Fitbit for the mind' to help people to maintain their focus of attention on a particular task? Could we develop a device that would alert people when they were being distracted, and that would provide appropriate, nuanced motivational feedback when they needed a bit of a boost?

As teachers, we are required to make judgements about the unseen mental processing that has produced particular observable behaviours in our students. We can also complement the behaviours that we observe with carefully designed formative assessment questions that we can ask students in order to reveal how they are progressing. And yet, as educators we know only too well that there are still many factors that will influence the learning of our students as a result of what happens in these students' lives beyond the tiny percentage of time that we spend with them. I don't mean by this statement that we need to start being nosy about the intimate details of our students' personal and social lives. I mean that we constantly need to contextualize our understanding of each student in a manner that would reflect their learning-relevant interactions in the world outside the class or lecture room. What happens to them beyond our time with them has a great impact on their learning, and if we can start to understand more about our students' contexts then we could probably increase the impact we have on their learning.

In May 2017, *The Economist* suggested that 'data is the oil of the digital era'. From CCTV to the ID cards that we swipe to get into our offices, that let us buy our lunch in the canteen, or enable us to log in to a computer system to download a book or interact with colleagues, our activity is captured as data streams that could be available for analysis. We voluntarily provide more data about ourselves through social media postings and our interactions with various software packages, audio interfaces such as Apple's Siri and Amazon's Alexa, and through a host of 'Internet of Things' devices – 'the network of physical devices, home appliances and other items embedded with electronics ... and connectivity which enables these objects to connect and share data' (Wikipedia, n.d.d.) – that we may have bought. The amount of data generated about ourselves has exploded, and most of the time we have no idea how it is being stored and processed in the cloud. This is all in addition to the data that we deliberately collect about our students and pupils through various educational platforms and applications.

However, in the same way that oil is crude and must be refined in various ways to produce a range of outputs, from petrol to plastic, so too must data be refined. This data refinement is where AI can help. The combination of large datasets and AI technology is where the really interesting work is happening. It is this combination of the right data with well-designed AI technology that will empower our human intelligence.

Big data and AI technology will empower our human intelligence

The interwoven intelligence model makes clear that no robot or AI is intelligent in the way that we humans are intelligent. Personally, I do not believe that AI will ever be intelligent in the ways that humans are intelligent, but there are many scientists who would disagree with this view. I will not venture further into the debate between those who do and do not believe in the singularity here, because there are many excellent accounts of these discussions (see Boden (2016) for an accessible summary). I will therefore confine my claim about the limitations of AI to the sorts of AI at the cutting edge of what we can currently achieve.

My judgement about the intelligence of current AI is based upon the seven core elements that I believe are essential for human intelligence, as outlined in Chapter 4. I do, however, believe that AI is already very powerful, and that its power is increasing rapidly. In terms of Element 1 of our interwoven intelligence, knowledge and understanding that is multidisciplinary and interdisciplinary, AI is a high achiever. It can perform tasks that involve processing large amounts of data far more quickly and accurately than the human mind. So how can we use this data processing power of AI on all the data we can now capture to develop more sophisticated intelligence of the sort that AI cannot achieve?

The answer is to be found in the process of designing good questions, initially discussed in Chapter 1. There, I highlighted the fact that AI is more than the technology that implements it; AI is about how we analyse problems and specify solutions. The way we analyse a problem for an AI to address is through asking the right questions. It is these questions that will drive the collection of good evidence from which we can make sound judgements that we can justify.

Designing the right question

The right question will lead to an answer that tells us what we want to know – but of course, we need to know what it is we want to know in order to ask the right question. For example, I may be concerned about my ability to plan my work schedule effectively with particular respect to my ability to plan sufficient time for marking student's work. If I break this down a little further, I may wish to find out if my ability to plan the time it takes me to mark my masters students' dissertations has improved, using data that I can access about my work patterns and so on. I will need to pose my question appropriately. In this instance, I might frame the question as follows: has the *difference* between the time I allocated to my marking and the time it actually takes me to complete my marking reduced over the last three years? I would then need to look at the available data sources to see if any of them will enable me to address this question. This would require, for example, information from my digital diary and, if I have marked the dissertations online, from the university's online marking system. I would need to have accurately recorded the time I allocated in my diary to marking and, if no online marking system exists, I would also need to have recorded the time I spent marking dissertations over the last three years. Nevertheless, despite this potential for error, my simple question about planning marking time is simple, and with some luck the data should be available, and the question should be answered fairly easily.

Suppose, then, that I discover I have got worse at estimating and planning my dissertation marking. The question I used to drive my analysis was not designed in a way that would provide any information to explain the diminishing quality of my planning skills. I need to think more carefully about the question that I have chosen to drive the way that I probe the data. In addition to basic information about my performance, we also need to find out information about the length of the dissertations, the number of dissertations, the complexity of the dissertation topics, the range of marks awarded, my familiarity with the work of the students, the time of day that I completed the marking, the last time that I had eaten ... the list is endless.

However, I could revise my original question as follows: what are the factors that have impacted upon my time planning for dissertation marking over the last three years? Now I will be driven by a question that requires far more complex processing. This is still a fairly simple question, but by answering many questions like this, we can collect component answers to build up a picture of my metacognitive planning skills.

There is a further substantial challenge that I must address in the way that I design the questions driving my data analysis. I need to have a preconceived idea about what success looks like. I need to understand my priorities, because it is insufficient merely to aim to increase the sophistication of my intelligence across all elements in an even sort of way. The interconnected nature of the intelligence elements means that improving my metacognitive knowledge, for example, may also improve my metacontextual knowledge, and vice versa. However, as I improve the sophistication of my metacognition and metacontextual knowledge, I may lose track of my emotions and therefore my metasubjective knowledge may reduce. I need a very clear view about what I want to achieve, and where my priorities are, in order to design the questions that I ask from my personal data.

Analogies to sport work quite well here, because the activities completed as part of sports training are mostly readily observable. One needs to bear in mind, of course, that a great deal of what we are talking about when it comes to intelligence is not as easy to observe as sports performance. Bearing that limitation in mind, I use a sports analogy to explain the importance of having a clear understanding of what we want to know from our data and why we want to know it.

A couple of years ago a young man came to see me because he wanted to ask for my help with his company's product. He was developing an adaptive learning system. This situation is not unusual; there are many people trying to develop good adaptive learning systems. However, this entrepreneur was a former professional tennis player, and he wanted to use the coaching methodology that he had benefited from in order to design the working of his adaptive learning system. As a professional tennis player his goal had been clear: it was to achieve the highest position in the world rankings that he could. To achieve this he needed to win matches. But that did not translate into a training regime that consisted merely of playing matches. His sleep and diet were tracked, he needed to be generally fit and spend considerable amounts of time in the gym, he had to ensure that his mental state was positive and that he was motivated. He needed to work on the components of his game: his serve, his backhand and his forehand. He needed to know what he was up against in the players that he was matched against. There were many elements to his coaching regime, but all the time he knew what success looked like, even though many of the elements in his coaching regime looked nothing like playing a tennis match. The system he developed (Performance Learning, n.d.) involved evaluating a wide range of learners' behaviours, from their sleep and diet to their resilience, confidence and persistence.

And so it is for us too, as we design the best way to use data and AI to help us increase the sophistication of our intelligence. We need a clear vision of what we want to achieve, and we need to know how we might get there. In educational terminology, the way we know we are making progress is called a progression model. I return to the subject of progression models when I discuss the implications of AI and the need to reconceptualize our intelligence in Chapter 6.

The questions that we ask of the data to find evidence about our intelligence must be grounded in our understanding of the intelligence that we are trying to identify. For example, the questions that we ask about Element 1 – our knowledge and understanding within and across subjects – will be very different from the questions we ask about our emotional relationship to that knowledge and understanding (Element 5).

The key question that we now need to answer in order to see how AI can help us develop our human intelligence, is as follows: how can we identify evidence about our development within and across the elements of our human intelligence within the masses of data that are collected as we interact in the world?

Before I go on to discuss how we might answer this question, there are some important issues about data that need to be considered.

Data issues
Where data comes from and where it goes
Data is all around. Throughout the technology-enabled world, there is little we can do that is not recorded through technology in some way. In theory, this means that there are huge amounts of data that we could use to help us understand more about the development of our intelligence. However, there are some significant ethical implications that cannot be ignored in any discussion about what data should be available about each of us, and to whom it should be available.

When Judy Kay and I were discussing the interfaces we wished to design for our personal analytics tools for both learners and teachers, we decided the only way to progress with the enterprise was to decide that, for the moment at least, these interfaces would be available only to the person whose data was being analysed and presented. The story of what had happened to the inBloom Center in the USA had given us serious cause for concern and highlighted that a great deal of work needs to be done to ensure that people are happy for their data to be used. The main aim of inBloom was to store, clean and aggregate a wide range of student information for individual US states. This clean data was then to be made available to approved third parties, who would develop tools so that the data could be easily used by classroom educators. However, many parents feared that the data collected could be used against their children. The initiative was shut down because of the public outcry (see McCambridge, 2014 for a fuller explanation). This experience should give us serious cause for concern and it highlights the fact that a great deal of work must be done to ensure that people are happy for their data to be used. In particular much is required to assure people regarding the use and processing of data about children, even when this processing has the aim of improving their children's education, as was the case with inBloom.

The aforementioned article in the *Economist* suggesting that data is the new oil also drew attention to the fact that the large technology companies who trade in data, such as Facebook, Amazon and Alphabet, are generating enormous amounts of power through their control of vast quantities of data. These companies have data about almost everyone in the digitally enabled world. This data is not valuable merely because it comes in huge quantities, but because of the way these companies process and refine it: to tell them what people are buying, what they are searching for and who they are connecting with.

The power accumulated in these companies must surely be addressed and reduced in order to avoid the inevitable monopolization of the personal data market and of data refinement. And yet, collecting, collating, refining and extracting meaning from data is also the mainstay of much work within the communities of academic researchers who process educational data with the help of AI. The latter community is hampered by a lack of investment and by their adherence to ethical standards and protocols. It is right that any educational application of AI must be ethically designed and approved; it is also right that much more investment should be made in the development of educational applications of AI. And it is right that the large technology companies should be required to adhere to the same standards of ethical regulation as research scientists.

The potential for the misuse of both personal data and the algorithms that process this data is huge. The lack of transparency about the personal data collected from people without their explicit *informed* permission will undermine confidence in AI as inevitable misuses come to light. Clearly these *informed* permissions can be achieved only if people are educated about AI and given the skills to influence AI's development. Another concern is the potential for bias (conscious or unconscious) to be incorporated into AI. As a society, we need to empower individual members of the public to take charge of their personal data; we need to show them how to harness this data for their own benefit and give them the tools to scrutinize the algorithms developed (or at least the decisions at which these algorithms arrive). The use of AI to process personal data must also be subjected to regulation to ensure that it is fair, and to guarantee transparency about what the processing is designed to achieve, even if the detail of how it is completed remains private for commercial reasons.

I will talk more in Chapter 6 about the need to educate people about AI. My purpose for including this discussion now is to draw attention to the fact that we need greater transparency and regulation of our personal data in order to ensure that it can be used to increase our human intelligence in the way I suggest here.

Data + AI = evidence

Let's assume that we can solve the problem of informed consent and persuade people that it is in their interests for us to access their data in order to tell them more about their intelligence and how they are developing it. We then need to decide what sort of AI technology might best help us to find the highest-quality evidence about the different elements of our intelligence and how we develop them.

I have already pointed out that in order to apply our chosen question to the available data we need to know what good evidence looks like. In other words, we need to know what intelligence looks like within and across all its elements. If we can specify how the different levels of intelligence sophistication can be recognized then we should be able to find evidence within our data. This sounds exactly like the sort of task that machine-learning AI is incredibly good at. We train our AI on data from people who are acknowledged as being intelligent within and/or across the seven intelligence elements, and then we set it free to find similar patterns in our data. The AI should improve as it processes more data and finds ever more similarities between people beyond those in the data of the people with which it was trained. It may even find patterns that we had never thought existed. This all sounds quite straightforward, although not necessarily simple.

There is, however, a major flaw in this plan. We need our AI to be able to explain why it has decided that the data it has analysed about a person provides evidence that the development of their intelligence within and across each element has a particular level of sophistication. If there is no explanation about why the AI has decided something about our intelligence, how can we know where we need to improve in order to increase the sophistication of our intelligence? For example, if an AI tells me that I only have a simple personal epistemology, how can I improve this without an associated explanation about why the evidence processed by the AI to date has led it to this conclusion?

This is the XAI problem that I discussed in Chapter 4. It is the reason why machine learning alone will not enable us to shed new light on our human intelligence. The work being done through the XAI research programme may change the situation, but for now at least we need to find a different approach.

A possible way forward is to be more specific about what we ask our machine learning AI to find in the data.

Signifiers of intelligence

Problem decomposition is the process of breaking down a complex problem into its constituent subproblems. It is a classic computing technique and one that is applied frequently by AI researchers to very good effect. Looking for information in data that will provide evidence about the particular elements of our intelligence is no exception as an example of the utility of this approach.

For instance, over the last few years I have worked with my colleagues Manolis Mavrikis and Mutlu Cukurova to investigate the sorts of evidence of student learning that can be identified through the careful analysis of multiple sorts of data. There are already good AI-driven software applications that track student performance in particular academic subjects – physics or mathematics for example. These systems do this by identifying evidence of success or evidence of errors in a student's interactions with the software as he or she works through problems and exercises. Mutlu, Manolis and I wanted to extend this work to situations where the activities students completed did not all use computer software. This would make the tools applicable to situations where students were working together to solve a problem or to complete a task, such as designing something: a toy or a new type of school bag, for example. We were interested in the challenge of identifying successful collaborative problem-solving behaviours. This is a more complex task than identifying evidence about learning a particular concept in physics from data about how students solve (or do not solve) a physics problem. Our ultimate aim was to design learning analytics that could be used to process data and provide teachers with more information about how their students were progressing in their collaborative problem-solving activities.

We knew that these learning analytics would need to work with data that had been collected in noisy classroom environments, so we could not rely on voice recognition and analysis. We therefore wanted to know if there were physical behaviours that we could identify from classroom data that were associated with any of the component parts of the collaborative problem-solving behaviours we had previously identified. So we asked the following two questions:

1. Are there observable differences between groups of students in the nonverbal and physical interactions they exhibit during collaborative problem-solving activity?
2. If there are differences, what aspects of nonverbal physical interactivity are good predictors of collaborative problem-solving performance?

The data that we had available to us was about the students' hand movements as they worked together to solve the problems, and data about the direction in which each student was looking at any particular moment in time.

Existing research evidence suggested that the synchrony of individual students' activities with each other could be a useful signifier of collaborative problem-solving performance (see, for example, Maldonado *et al.* (2007). We therefore designed research questions that entailed searching the data for evidence related to the synchrony in our students' hand movements and gaze direction. We probed the data to see if we could identify synchrony of behaviour, and to explore if this synchrony varied in accordance with the students' collaborative problem-solving performance. The evidence from our research indicated that the students who were rated by an independent human evaluator as demonstrating a high level of collaborative problem-solving efficacy also demonstrated high-levels of hand and gaze synchrony with their peers. We concluded that the respective synchrony of student hand movements and gaze direction could be considered as signifiers of collaborative problem-solving behaviour. We needed to do more research, but there was enough evidence for us to believe that this research would be fruitful.

The work that Mutlu, Manolis and I conducted could be described as data science. Data science is a fast-growing area of research, involving analysis of our behaviour as buyers and our voting preferences in elections. Data science that is concerned with intellectual development would generally fall within the realms of educational data mining or learning analytics research. There is much work from within these research communities that can be useful for the identification of signifiers and analytical techniques to probe our human intelligence across all its elements.

Researchers who work as part of the educational data mining and learning analytics community analyse large educational datasets, usually in order to make predictions about the future. I will discuss this work in greater detail in Chapter 6, which focuses on education. Here, within this discussion about signifiers, it is useful to note that educational data mining has been developing new tools to identify patterns within data. Likewise learning analytics employs automated analysis, but also considers human intervention to analyse datasets.

The task of designing the signifiers that will tell us what we need to know about our intelligence and that we can use to help both our students and ourselves to develop our intelligence is an enormous task. However, this task can be broken down into its component parts: designing the right questions, identifying the available data, and designing the signifiers that can be extracted from the data to answer the questions.

We might conclude that we could reframe our original question about how we identify evidence concerning the elements of our human intelligence within the data collected about our interactions in the world. A new possible framing could be as follows: What are the signifiers of our intelligent development that can be found within the available data about our interactions in the world?

Signifiers are the outputs from analysed data that can be interpreted as evidence that a particular behaviour has been identified in that data. Signifiers can be simple or they can be complex, composed of multiple simple signifiers. They can use and combine raw data, and different signifiers can be constructed from different combinations of processed data. For example, the data about student hand movements produces simple signifiers of the synchrony of the hand movements between a group of students. If we combine this simple signifier with another simple signifier about student gaze direction, then we can formulate a complex signifier that we hope will tell us something about a small facet of collaborative problem-solving behaviour.

Once we have a set of signifiers that we have validated through empirical studies, we can use it as training data for machine-learning AI, which can then quickly process the huge amounts of data about our interactions and find the signifiers in this data. Once we have a set of signifiers we can use other AI techniques to build dynamic computer models of the different elements of our intelligence and the interactions between them. We can visualize these dynamic computer models through well-designed interfaces that help us to interact with these models in the way that Judy and I had envisaged for our iPALs and iPATs. However, the presentation of this information about our intelligence is not enough on its own to help us increase the sophistication within and across the seven elements of human intelligence. We need to apply what we know about how people learn, and how good teachers teach, to develop the support that will help us use the information about our intelligence that AI and big data can provide.

But what about the 'Fitbit for the mind', you might reasonably ask? This talk of signifiers within and across all seven elements of our intelligence sounds far too complex for a Fitbit analogy to be appropriate. The usefulness of the 'Fitbit for the mind' analogy, and of any such device should it be developed, will depend upon our ability to identify the right priorities to track about our intelligence. I suspect that different people – and indeed the same person at different times in life – would like to prioritize different aspects of their intelligence. I believe that accurate perceived self-efficacy might be a useful place to focus our attention if we want a universally useful proxy for intelligence development. Accurate perceived self-efficacy may be akin to the 'steps' that the many fitness devices use: a sort of common currency for intelligence fitness.

Summary

In this chapter I have explored the implications of an interwoven intelligence model that differentiates us from robots and other AI technologies. My aim has been to demonstrate how the technology of AI can help humans to increase the sophistication of their intelligence. The AI technologies cannot themselves produce the rich repertoire of intelligence available to humans. This is mainly because AI does not understand itself, cannot explain or justify its decisions, and has no self-awareness. However, the combination of voluminous data and well-designed AI can help us as humans to track the way in which our intelligence is developing. If we can track the development of our intelligence then we can use what we know about learning and existing educational techniques, and we can develop new techniques to improve our intelligence continually in ways that are unavailable to robots and AIs. We can provide people with a 'way in' to understanding their intelligence – in a similar way to how people who had not previously been able to engage with understanding their fitness and relating it to the exercise they did were given a 'way in' through devices like the Fitbit and Misfit. Can we perhaps help people to understand the development of all the elements of their intelligence by giving them a 'way in' through AI?

I have discussed the different fears and beliefs of people working in different jobs as revealed by the ABC television programme *The AI Race*. Their lack of curiosity about how they might better prepare themselves for AI's onslaught on their workplace surprised me and led me to conclude that I needed to write a sort of self-help book for the AI age. When looking for successful self-help books I stumbled across *Who Moved My Cheese?*. Reading this book helped me to frame seven messages that we humans might do well to consider.

The dilemma of AI is both beautiful and dangerous. We have created AI technology in our own image of intelligence and, in the process, we have diminished our valuation of our own intelligence. But, we can use AI to help us develop our human intelligence beyond the ways in which our AI technology can develop its own intelligence. We can collect data about our every word, movement and action. We can use our AI technology to process this data, to look for patterns in it that represent the development of our human intelligence repertoire, to tell us more about ourselves and our intellectual development. To design the AI to process all our data in a useful way, we need to know the right questions to ask of the data. However, the AI will not be able to explain its analysis, and we therefore need to use our human intelligence to design appropriate signifiers that AI can look for in our data. The signifiers can then be used as the building blocks of our intelligence analysis, through which we can identify progress and explain what makes us the type of intelligent that we want to be.

Well-designed and combined signifiers might help us to track our intellectual development in a similar way to how we track our fitness. However, we need to decide what priorities should drive our intelligence tracking. For example, perceived self-efficacy could be a useful priority for most people and something that might act as a focus for intelligence tracking in the same way that 'steps' provide a useful focus for fitness tracking for the majority of people.

In Chapter 6 I will consider the implications of using AI to help humans to move with the intelligence, so that they do not languish in outdated definitions. If we get our education systems right, we need never feel we are intelligent enough: we can use AI to help us to keep striving for intellectual growth.

The power of learning and the importance of education

Learning is the holy grail of success and intelligence. If we are good at learning, the world is our oyster and we can continually progress. Learning is also what sets modern AI aside from the earlier so-called Good Old-Fashioned AI (GOFAI). GOFAI was the name adopted by John Haugeland in his 1985 book *Artificial Intelligence: The Very Idea*. It refers to the AI techniques that were used prior to the adoption of neural networks. The reason that the AI system AlphaGo beat master Go player Lee Sedol in March 2016 (Wikipedia, n.d.a.) is that AlphaGo was phenomenally good at learning. If we are to *move* intelligence in the way that I have argued in Chapter 5 that we must, then our ability to learn is the key to our success. Learning is what helps us to develop our intelligence across and between all of the elements I described in Chapter 4. We must use our education and training system to ensure that learning is what everyone can do well.

Learning for an AI world

In my discussion of Vygotsky's zone of proximal development (ZPD) in Chapter 1, I described how it is intended to identify the interactions between people that will have the greatest impact upon their development and intelligence. These are the interactions that we, as teachers, must foster. We must also engage both the System 1 and the System 2 minds of our students, and of ourselves. Our algorithmic and rational System 2 minds accommodate our intellect, but System 2 is inherently lazy, and is lost without the instinctive System 1 mind (Kahneman, 2011). System 1 includes a range of valuable abilities. It is the home of the *learned associations* that we can increase through rehearsal, and of our abilities to recognize objects, detect how other people are feeling and read simple text. The behaviours that are manifested through the mental processing of System 1 are not generally under our control, and may appear to occur automatically, but in reality, they are the result of much practice and they are fundamental to the richness of our human intelligence.

Education systems therefore need to embrace teaching that addresses the needs of both the System 1 and System 2 minds of students. This would be teaching that respects what System 1 has to offer while also keeping it at bay, and sparking into action the behaviours of System 2. Such teaching will help learners to progress their learning and intelligence most effectively. In particular, education systems must encourage teachers to pay particular attention to developing the modestly named *rational* subsystem of the System 2 minds, because this is the subsystem that allows people to ignore their biases, and to keep the energetic attention-needing toddler that is each person's System 1 mind under control. In chapters 2 and 3 I linked our rational subsystem minds with the concept of self-efficacy, and stressed that both of these subsystems are fundamental to human intelligence. We diminish the intelligence potential of our students if we overvalue the algorithmic mind to the detriment of the rational. A well-developed and powerful rational subsystem is also a better predictor of ability than the traditional intelligence tests that only measure the powers of System 2's algorithmic subsystem.

My starting proposition, therefore, as we look at education and training in an increasingly AI-augmented world, is that we must design education and training using progression models that constantly promote growth across and between all elements of our intelligence. To do this successfully such progression models must acknowledge several facets of our minds: (1) the instinctive mental processing that enables us to automate certain knowledge and skills through practice, (2) the algorithmic process that helps us to develop sophisticated, knowledgeable understanding and skills, and (3) the rational meta-level processing that helps us to develop a knowledgeable understanding of ourselves. The progression model that we use for our education and training would also act as the foundation for assessment, for measuring the various elements of intelligence development. However, before we can deal with progression models and how we evaluate our success at learning, we first need to think about what we should be learning, and therefore what we should be teaching.

What should we learn?

The findings from the analysis reported in the ABC programme *The AI Race* to which I referred in Chapter 5 were clear. The narrative of the programme stressed that we must take advantage of what AI has to offer by *increasing the diversity of our own skill sets*. The programme suggested that AI could be an 'Iron Man suit' for people: a suit that would transform we mere humans into superhumans. This is a great analogy – who would not want to be superhuman? But embracing AI-augmented working is not as simple as putting on a new outfit – even an iron outfit. The change required to what and how we learn, teach and train, and to the way that we train our educators is enormous. It is impossible to make such a transformation in short order. We therefore need to consider carefully how we manage the transition from where we are now to the situation in which widespread AI augmentation will be commonplace.

Firstly, we need a much clearer specification of what it is we now need to teach and train people to be able to do. What are the knowledge and skills that people need to be effective at if they are to thrive in our AI augmented future? Secondly, increasing the diversity of our knowledge and skill sets requires educators and trainers who are themselves knowledgeable, skilled and trained in developing this new curriculum. Yet we already have a global teacher shortage, so where are these educators and trainers to be found? Who is helping the educators and trainers to gain the new knowledge, skills and expertise they will need to train their students?

Now we hit the nub of the matter: education and educators must prepare students for the new AI order of things. *Educators' lives are going to change in significant ways, not because their roles are likely to be automated away but because they will need to teach a different curriculum and probably teach in a different way.* To make matters worse, there is no clear consensus from the experts about exactly which jobs educators will need to educate people for. This is where I believe the interwoven intelligence model can be useful in guiding us towards understanding the intelligence that we need to develop in people.

Education for an AI-augmented world

What is the knowledge and which are the skills that people will need to understand in our AI-augmented future? To answer this question, I focus on one interpretation of the question 'Who moved my intelligence?', mooted in Chapter 4. I consider how we need to 'move' our students' intelligence beyond the routine cognitive processing of academic subject matter to encompass all seven of the elements in the interwoven intelligence model. Here again, for easy reference, are the seven points that made up my messages for 'Who moved my intelligence?'

1. Change happens: *They keep making smarter, more powerful computers*
2. Anticipate change: *Get ready for ever more powerful AI systems*
3. Monitor change: *Keep checking on your own intelligence to make sure you are keeping it fresh*

4. Adapt to change thoughtfully: *The more carefully you offload human intelligence to AI, the more AI can help you educate for sophisticated human intelligence*
5. Change: *Move with the new potential for diversifying human intelligence*
6. Enjoy change! *Savour the journey and enjoy new ways to develop sophisticated human intelligence among more students*
7. Be ready to change and enjoy developing human intelligence again: *They keep making smarter, more powerful computers*

There are many versions of the so-called 21st century skills that we need to instil in people. Most versions have some things in common; there are also always a few differences. For example, in 2015 the World Economic Forum published a report called *New Visions of Education: Unlocking the potential of technology.* This report divided 21st century skills into three categories:

- *Foundational literacies* would equip students to apply their core skills to everyday tasks. These included conventional literacy, numeracy, scientific literacy, ICT literacy, financial literacy, and cultural and civic literacy.
- *Competencies* would help students approach complex challenges. Four competencies were identified: critical thinking and problem-solving, creativity, communication and collaboration.
- *Character qualities* would help students know how to approach their changing environments. There were six character qualities: curiosity, initiative, persistence, adaptability, leadership and social and cultural awareness.

By contrast, Bernie Trilling and Charles Fadel, in a much-cited book entitled *21st Century Skills: Learning for Life in our Times* (Trilling and Fadel, 2009), suggested a slightly different set of capabilities. Like the World Economic Forum, Trilling and colleagues categorized 21st century skills into three groups:

- *Learning and innovation skills.* Learning to create together. This category included the 'knowledge and skills rainbow', learning to learn and innovate, critical thinking and problem-solving, communication and collaboration, creativity and innovation.
- *Digital literacy skills.* This category included information literacy, media literacy and ICT literacy.

- *Career and life skills* included flexibility and adaptability, initiative and self-direction, social and cross-cultural interaction, productivity and accountability, and leadership and responsibility.

These two examples illustrate the lack of consensus among those who are attempting to identify these skills. All of the skills suggested sound like good ideas, but they do not together provide a good basis for designing education and training systems. There is an additional problem with these approaches, and that lies in the word 'skill'. There is a ferocious and ongoing debate (see, for example, Wheelahan, 2015; Christodoulou, 2014; Grist, 2009) between those educators who believe that we should be helping students to become skilled in various different ways, and those who believe that knowledge is the only way forward and should therefore be our primary focus in helping our students to acquire knowledge. Personally, I think this is a rather overblown debate and even a red herring, because knowledge and skills cannot really be separated. We need knowledge in order to become skilled, and we need skills in order to acquire knowledge. I will therefore sidestep this debate by focusing on the seven elements of intelligence that I presented in Chapter 4 and stress that we need both knowledgeable skills and skilful knowledge. For ease of reference, the definition for each element in Table 4.1 is given here in a box below the relevant heading.

Element 1: Academic intelligence

Knowledge about the world. Knowledge and understanding that is multi- and interdisciplinary. Knowledge is not the same as information, but we frequently muddle them up. We need to stop doing this.

The ability to construct interdisciplinary knowledge and to apply this understanding to the world is fundamental to developing a deep understanding, and is very much at the forefront of many education systems in the world today. The changes that need to be made to many of our education systems in order to ensure that interwoven intelligence Element 1 is addressed are as much to do with *how* we teach as *what* we teach.

There are many excellent educational texts that offer good advice about how to teach a curriculum that is focused upon subject-specific knowledge and skills (see, for example, Atwell, 2007; Brown *et al.*, 2014; Gattegno, 1974; Husbands and Pearce, 2012; Lakatos *et al.*, 1976; Rosenshine, 2012). There are also some useful texts that deal with how interdisciplinary knowledge and skills can be taught (see, for example,

Beane, 1997; Boomer *et al.*, 1992; Chandramohan and Fallows, 2009; Jackson and Davis, 2000; Wood, 1997).

One book that has had considerable leverage in the UK in determining policy and curriculum for schools is Daisy Christodoulou's (2014) *Seven Myths about Education*. The first myth that Christodoulou identifies is that 'Facts prevent understanding'. She takes her evidence for why facts are important for understanding from cognitive science and, interestingly, from early work in AI. She adopts the constrained definition of intelligence originally proposed by John Anderson (1996): 'all that there is to intelligence is the simple accrual and tuning of many small units of knowledge that in total produce complex cognition. The whole is no more than the sum of its parts, but it has a lot of parts' (Christodoulou, 2014: 356).

Christodoulou's argument is not aimed at criticising true conceptual understanding and higher-order skill development, which she acknowledges are the aims of education. She is rather concerned to argue that facts and subject content are not opposed to such aims, and that they are rather a part of it. She suggests that scholars like Rousseau, Dewey and Freire were wrong to see facts as the enemy of understanding. In her defence of facts, Christodoulou cites Herb Simon (1996; also in collaboration with Anderson *et al.*, 1995) and John Sweller (Sweller and Sweller, 2006), as well as John Anderson – all researchers I came across in my early studies of AI at Sussex. Her recommendations about teaching facts revolve around the way that we can use our long-term memory to help out our limited working memory. We can only do this, however, if we have committed the rules and information to that long-term memory by learning things by rote. For example, we can chunk information, using background knowledge and rules stored in long-term memory.

I am happy to agree that there is a role for learning facts in education, and that higher-order skills such as creativity and problem-solving can be assisted through large bodies of knowledge that have been committed securely to memory. However, facts are only a small part of what our human intelligence can achieve and their importance should not be overplayed. Education systems that promote facts and teaching through drill and practice alone address solely our System 1 mind, and elements of the algorithmic subsystem of our System 2 minds. And yet, as we have discussed in chapters 1 and 5, it is the rational subsystem of our System 2 mind that we need to power up, if we are to develop sophisticated intelligence.

Element 1 intelligence that is at the heart of the knowledge-based curriculum will not be sufficient to help us outwit the robots. Rather it will open the door and welcome in our AI peers to take over more than is wise, because they will surely be better at this than we will ever be. For example, a new core part of the primary and secondary English curriculum in England (Department for Education, 2014) requires students to identify and name elements of grammar in a sentence when learning about reading and writing in their first language. That knowledge reveals nothing of the richness in the text and can be a distraction from the sort of intelligent, emotional interaction with text that matters and that is flexible with context or idiom.

A parallel example from primary mathematics would be the requirement for students to recall the prime numbers up to 100. Identifying prime numbers, which can be a mere memory exercise, overlooks the mystery and beauty of the number system that, again, invokes an emotional response in humans. Why else would the notion of 'lucky numbers' exist within many cultures around the world? Just knowing the prime numbers does little to help students appreciate their wide applications in areas such as cryptography.

There is a second reason why approaches such as that suggested by Christodoulou are dangerous for our future education systems. This danger is related to the fact that the knowledge-based curriculum is founded on studies of memory – working and long-term – and on early models of learning developed by AI researchers. As such, it is building a curriculum in the same way that we build AI systems and playing to the strengths of AI, rather than to the strengths of human intelligence. This second danger is the other side of the coin to the danger of continuing to focus our education system on what AI does best, and thus failing to differentiate human intelligence in all its splendour.

AI AND ELEMENT 1

AI is brilliant at performing the routine cognitive skills of knowledge acquisition. The information that can be processed and learned by readily available machine-learning systems are way beyond our human capability. The capacity for knowledge learning and acquisition held by systems such as IBM's Watson far outstrips what we can achieve (see Ferrucci, 2012; Whitney, 2017). Watson can process vast amounts of information, remember it and then retrieve it as and when required extremely quickly. It is able to access vast amounts of information from publications including blogs, newspapers and reports. The AI within Watson uses natural language processes to analyse all this written information grammatically, relationally and structurally to extract meaning. For any particular domain – medicine or finance, for example – Watson's AI uses this processing to learn the language of that domain and to build a corpus of knowledge about it, which it then indexes and curates. Watson is then trained to solve problems and answer questions by matching the problem it is asked to solve with the information it has processed. For example, we might ask Watson for simple factual information, such as which king was killed at the Battle of Hastings in 1066 – but we can also ask much more sophisticated questions, such as what is the best way to treat someone who is suffering from anxiety. In this case Watson will search through its corpus of knowledge to match the details of the individual person who is suffering from anxiety with possible treatment plans within this corpus. It will search within this corpus too for evidence about the efficacy of different treatment options.

This AI capability is both a serious concern and a possible solution to the problem of teaching knowledge in our schools and colleges. It is this capability for learning and acquiring knowledge that means that AI systems can help us humans to develop some of this knowledge, and to learn some of these facts.

It is relatively straightforward to develop AI systems that can teach well-defined subject areas, such as those that are routinely part of the STEM curriculum. These systems can help learners to build an understanding of the facts that remain a part of STEM subject curricula. They can help with deeper study of these subjects too, thus linking to other intelligences and helping to build stepping stones that will develop a learner's personal epistemology. Some of these AI systems are modelled on research by AI scientists, such as Anderson, Simon and Sweller – research that is also the basis for the what and how of teaching proposed by Christodoulou.

These systems, such as those developed by Carnegie Learning (n.d.), provide individualized tutoring by continually assessing each student's progress. The assessment process is underpinned by an AI-enabled computer model of the mental processes that produce successful and near-successful student performance. The growing body of AI educators is increasingly breaking beyond the constrained areas of STEM subjects, to language learning for example, with companies such as Alelo (2018) developing culture and language-learning products that specialize in experiential digital learning driven by virtual role-play simulations powered by AI. Machine learning techniques are also being used to enable companies such as UK-based Century Tech (2018) to develop a learning platform, with input from neuroscientists, that tracks students' interactions, including every mouse movement and each keystroke. Century's AI looks for patterns and correlations in the data from the student, their year group, and their school to offer a personalized learning journey for the student. It also provides teachers with a dashboard, giving them a real-time snapshot of the learning status of every child in their class. There is now every chance that an AI educator can be developed for almost all areas of the current school and college curriculum in most countries. Therefore, if we reduce the job of teaching to one of helping students remember facts and rules and using these alone to construct key knowledge across school or college subject areas, we are damning teachers to be replaced by AI.

We must be far more ambitious for our learners than merely helping them to acquire knowledgeable understanding and skills from the standard academic curriculum. All educators know that this has never been sufficient. But, because we can now increasingly leave the job of doing this Element 1 development to AI, we must develop education systems that encourage our human educators to use their expertise to focus on the other elements of our human intelligence.

Element 2: Social intelligence

Social interaction capabilities. Social interaction is the basis of individual thought and of communal intelligence. AI cannot achieve human-level social interaction. There is also a meta-aspect to social intelligence through which we can develop an awareness of and the ability to regulate our own social interactions.

There are many arguments within the AI community about exactly what AI is, and what it can and cannot achieve, both now and in the future. These are eloquently discussed by Max Tegmark (2017). However, there is an overall agreement that social interaction is not something at which AI excels. It is, however, something at which humans *can* excel. It is the responsibility of governments to ensure that educational and training policies provide appropriate opportunities for social interaction to help students build an advanced knowledgeable understanding of the world. This is important both for the individual intellectual development of each person and for the development of our communal intelligence. This communal intelligence can be greater than the sum of its parts, and it can also differentiate us from AI.

Social interaction can be challenging in formal education and training settings. Educators recognize its importance, but it is not always recognized in the curriculum or by regulators. Perhaps as a result, it is less common in practice than one might expect. For example, Galton *et al.* (1999) found that children who were sitting in small groups for the vast majority of time were involved in collaborative learning activity for only about 14 per cent of that time. Similar patterns were reported in UK schools (among students aged 5 to 16 years) by Baines *et al.* (2003) and by Kutnick and Blatchford

(2013), and in findings reported in other countries (for a US illustration see Webb and Palincsar, 1996). The OECD TALIS (2013) survey also reinforces the finding that collaborative approaches are rare. Findings indicate that on average across the 34 countries surveyed, 8 per cent of teachers said that they use small groups in all or nearly all of their lessons, while only 40 per cent said they used them frequently.

In a report published by Nesta (Luckin *et al.*, 2017), the following barriers to the widespread uptake of collaborative problem-solving were identified:

- There is a disparity between collaborative problem-solving and the prevailing exam-driven education system and curriculum.
- Collaborative problem-solving is not easy for teachers to implement amid heavy workloads and high-risk demands on their time and skills.
- Teachers can be sceptical about the benefits of collaborative problem-solving. Teachers report loss of control, increased disruption and off-task behaviour as the main reasons for avoiding collaborative problem-solving and learning in the classroom (Cohen, 1994).
- Teachers have little training or confidence in undertaking collaborative learning within their classrooms (Kutnick *et al.*, 2005).
- Students may lack collaborative problem-solving skills and there is uncertainty about the capacity of students to work together (Lewis and Cowie, 1993).
- Students have concerns about collaborative problem-solving: working with peers can be a risky and emotionally stressful experience, which may result in squabbles, enduring conflicts and public embarrassment (Järvenoja and Järvelä, 2013); some children may not like working with others.

A lovely example of a project that worked with teachers to develop a programme to improve the effectiveness of collaborative group work among children aged 5 to 14 years can be found in the SPRinG programme (see Baines *et al.*, 2016). Research findings showed that engaging in the SPRinG programme had a positive effect on all pupils, with marked gains in attainment and learning, and changes in pupil behaviour and interaction that explained changes in attainment and learning (Blatchford *et al.*, 2006). Teachers also reported positive effects for both their practice and classroom management and for their students. The SPRinG approach is structured around four key principles for facilitating collaboration:

- Careful attention to the physical and social organization of the classroom and groups (e.g. taking account of the number, size, stability and composition of groups).
- Development of pupils' group-working skills (based upon an inclusive relational approach, working with all children in a class) through activities to develop social, communication and advanced group-working skills.
- The creation and structuring of challenging tasks that legitimise collaborative group work.
- The supportive involvement of teachers and other adults in guiding, facilitating and monitoring collaborative group work.

It is extremely difficult to isolate the precise nature of the key factors that affect the effectiveness or otherwise of collaborative problem-solving. We can, however, identify factors that are frequently mentioned as being influential upon success. These factors include the environment in which collaborative problem-solving takes place; the composition, stability and size of the group and their problem-solving and social skills; and teacher training (Cukurova *et al.*, 2018).

As reported in Luckin *et al.* (2017), to be effective at collaborative problem-solving, people must be able to:

- articulate, clarify and explain their thinking;
- re-structure, clarify and, in the process, strengthen their own understanding and ideas to develop their awareness of what they know and what they do not know;
- adjust their explanations when presenting their thinking, which requires that they can also estimate others' understandings;
- listen to ideas and explanations from others – this may lead listeners to develop understanding in areas that were hitherto missing from their own knowledge;
- elaborate and internalize their new understanding as they process the ideas they hear about from others;
- actively engage in the construction of ideas and thinking as part of the co-construction of understandings and solutions;
- resolve conflicts and respond to challenges by providing complex explanations, counterevidence and counterarguments; and
- search for new information to resolve the internal cognitive conflict that arises from discrepancies in the conceptual understanding of others.

Collaborative problem-solving was considered important enough to be added to the OECD's PISA assessment programme in 2015. When the results were published, towards the end of 2017, Andreas Schleicher (the OECD director for education and skills) urged educational systems to do better in helping their students to develop these skills (OECD, 2017).

The PISA results illustrated that those who perform most strongly in other PISA assessments in science, reading and mathematics also tend to perform well in the collaborative problem-solving assessment. However, the results also highlighted a cause for concern across the world. They reflected a lack of high-level collaborative problem-solving skills among students from all countries, including those that performed the best. Even students in Singapore struggled with the more advanced demands of collaborative problem-solving, with little more than 20 per cent of students able to attain the advanced level 4 in their PISA collaborative problem-solving assessment. This suggests that there remains a great deal of work for educators to do if we are to ensure that people have knowledge and skills that they can apply effectively when working with others in the workplace.

There is of course another reason why collaborative problem-solving is so important: it requires the ability to justify decision-making. This is almost impossible for AI systems because, while they work together, they are not able to synthesize their various domain-specific intelligences and so are not able to justify their decisions.

In summary, social intelligence is at the core of both individual and communal human intelligence. The provision of appropriate opportunities for social interaction is the responsibility of policymakers and educators, and it needs to receive a larger profile in many education systems. Social interaction, for example, in the form of collaborative problem-solving, is a good way of teaching and learning, if it is done properly in a structured and well-planned manner. We therefore need to train our educators to use social intelligence effectively and appropriately in their practice.

AI AND ELEMENT 2
It is difficult, probably impossible, for AI to achieve collaborative problem-solving. Different AI systems can work together, but they are not able to interact socially, nor are they able to justify their decisions – two key requirements for good collaborative problem-solvers. This means that while AI can perform well at some aspects of the problem-solving parts of collaborative problem-solving, operating in ways such as those described in the earlier discussions of Watson, it cannot accomplish the whole collaborative problem-solving process.

AI can, however, support humans to learn to be better at working together to solve problems. Several approaches to the use of AI for collaborative learning have been investigated, including adaptive group formation, expert facilitation, virtual agents and intelligent moderation (Luckin *et al.*, 2016). For example, Vizcaíno (2005) developed an intelligent virtual agent that acted as a virtual peer, an artificial student who was operating at a similar level of understanding to the learners being taught. Virtual-agent students like this can be used to introduce new ideas, provide information clarification or to motivate the student. Artificially intelligent agents can also play the role of an expert or mentor to a group of students. A slightly different approach is adopted in a system call Betty's Brain (Vanderbilt University, 2014). In this system, human students can engage in working together to teach an artificially intelligent virtual student who may need to be helped to correct a misconception, for example.

We now consider the meta-intelligence elements (elements 3 to 7).

Element 3: Meta-knowing intelligence

Knowing about knowledge. Epistemic intelligence, or our personal epistemology: we must develop an understanding of what knowledge is, what it means to know something, what good evidence is and how to make judgements based on that evidence and our context.

A sophisticated personal epistemology involves us in learning to recognize what good evidence is and how to make judgements based on that evidence in order to construct our knowledge. Our personal epistemology is core to our perception of what it means to know and understand something, and it will help us to master Element 1 intelligence.

However, the question of how we bootstrap ourselves to an advanced and sophisticated personal epistemology is not straightforward. The evidence I discussed in Chapter 2 illustrated that even Harvard undergraduates can have a very simple personal epistemology. We cannot expect our students to develop greater sophistication without considerable support from educators and trainers.

My experience of teaching programming to undergraduate students taught me that I needed to simplify the initial concepts that I introduced to them in order to 'bootstrap' their ability to tackle something more complex. I therefore suggest that it is acceptable *initially* to allow students to work within a simple personal epistemology within which they believe in some objective reality that is knowledge. However, this must be *merely a stepping stone* on the way to a more sophisticated understanding. Our relationship with the objective reality notion of knowledge should be seen simply as something that will enable us to gather together a sort of factual literacy, which we can use as the foundation for further development. In the same way that Vygotsky suggested that the everyday concepts of our experience were fundamental to our development of higher-order thinking, and Daniel Kahneman showed how our automatic System 1 mind is essential to our intellectual System 2 mind, this basic factual literacy may be essential to the development of sophisticated personal epistemologies.

The process through which we extend the initially simple personal epistemologies of our students will need to recognize that their views about the source of knowledge and about how knowledge is justified will vary both within and across subject areas. If we are to instil in them an interdisciplinary knowledge and understanding, then they (and their educators) will also need an appreciation of the incoherence and inconsistency of their developing epistemology.

The study conducted by my PhD student Katerina, discussed in Chapter 2, also highlighted evidence that people are often very poor at articulating what they believe, and in particular why they believe it. For example, the undergraduates taking part in Katerina's study would state that knowledge was uncertain, but they would not be able to express why they believed this. This finding implies that students may report views that suggest a more sophisticated personal epistemology than will be evidenced through their practice. There are clear implications for assessment here.

The findings from Katerina's research were consistent with previous research studies (see Avramides, 2009) in demonstrating that students' views about the nature of knowledge are, at least initially, influenced by teaching. In particular, the way that material is presented to students will impact upon how they draw conclusions about its certainty, authority or ambiguity. Understandably students are more likely to accept and adopt the perspectives they are presented with by their teachers than they are to reject or even to question them.

Questioning the views presented by a teacher is not something that is always encouraged. We therefore need to be aware of the manner in which we assert intellectual authority through the subjects we teach. We also need to be aware that our intellectual dominance may be reducing our students' ability to synthesize critically across multiple viewpoints in order to construct their own knowledge and understanding. Katerina's study also concurred with other research about the importance of context: students' views about knowledge and its sources demonstrated that their understanding was tied to specific contexts. This finding should alert us to the need for caution when considering any evaluation of our students' personal epistemology, because decontextualized evaluations are doomed to inaccuracy. We will need to consider not just the views that students express but the evidence that is demonstrated through their contextualized actions.

One excellent example of how we can help students to develop a more sophisticated personal epistemology is through the process of debating. For example, Scott (2008) found that the debate process helped students both to gain disciplinary knowledge and to analyse and present arguments. D'Souza (2013) found that learning through debates facilitated learning in depth. The formal process of debating about a particular topic, in which opposing arguments are put forward in front of an audience who are then invited to vote, has been part of the education system for many decades. For example, Princeton University in the USA formed its influential American Whig society in 1769. The University of St Andrews in Scotland was the first in Great Britain to form a student debating society in 1794, followed closely by the Cambridge Union Society, which was founded in 1815 and claims to be the oldest continuously operating debating society in the world (Cambridge Union, 2018). Debate practice within the education system is mostly restricted to the independent school sector and some universities. However, a UK-based charity called Debate Mate provides a unique programme that uses debate to teach and to tackle the UK's chronic lack of social mobility. Students are taught to debate through debate clubs and master the ability to collate evidence to justify or falsify a debate proposition. They must marshal and communicate their evidence effectively, even when they do not personally agree with the position they are required to adopt. The programme is inclusive, fun, gender-balanced, sustainable and highly effective, and has been shown to accelerate student progress irrespective of background. The curriculum develops the whole person first: it teaches ideas thinking and employability skills, the human capacities that are at a premium because they cannot be automated. Since 2008, Debate Mate has educated over 50,000 young people, 5,000 professionals and 1,500 teachers in over 25 countries. They provide training courses for teachers so that they can start their own debate clubs and integrate debating into their curriculum (Debate Mate, 2018).

AI AND ELEMENT 3

The DARPA initiative to find ways to make AI technology explainable so that its decisions can be justified (discussed in Chapter 4) highlights the fact that a sophisticated personal epistemology is something that AI, in particular machine learning, does not possess. Howerver, AI systems, such as IBM Watson, do have the ability to collate large bodies of evidence and to select those sources with the greatest weight and authority. The accuracy of the results will depend upon the information that has been made available to Watson's AI and the training data and algorithms that have been used to help Watson collate, structure and learn. The Watson AI does not, however, understand what knowledge is and would not be good at debating itself. It could, however, be a useful aid for human debaters, and it could also be a useful tool to help us to learn how to ask good questions to get the best results from our AI.

A nice example that draws out the distinction between AI and human intelligence was provided by Yoam Shoaham at the ninth Ambassadors' Roundtable on Artificial Intelligence, on 27 February 2018 at the Royal Society in London. Shoaham illustrated one of the limitations of AI through the following sentence:

> *Mummy, Danny hit me at school so I hit him back. The teacher only saw me hitting him so she punished me. It's not fair.*

A child can understand this but AI cannot. It is too complex with respect to the roles played by different people, some of whom know things that others don't, and some people know that others do not know those things, while others don't. There are issues of fairness and indeed we could frame a debate around the appropriateness of the teacher's actions. An AI would struggle to join in such a debate, but humans would be great at it, and they can learn to be even better. This is a contrast to the situation with factual knowledge and information, where AI can beat us at learning hands down. When it comes to debating, however, and justification and explanation, we humans can beat AI hands down.

A sophisticated personal epistemology is important because it helps us develop more sophisticated knowledgeable understanding and skills from our academic studies. A sophisticated personal epistemology is also something that AI is not (yet) capable of achieving.

Element 4: Metacognitive intelligence

Includes regulation skills. We need to learn and develop the ability to interpret our own ongoing mental activity, and these interpretations need to be grounded in good evidence about our contextualized interactions in the world.

Metacognitive knowledge and regulation skills are the elements of intelligence that enable us to interpret and manage our own ongoing mental activity effectively. In the same way that our subject knowledge and skills are intertwined, metacognitive knowledge is intertwined with the metacognitive skills that help us to regulate how we use our metacognitive knowledge. Metacognition needs to be learnt, developed, encouraged and supported.

We can think of our regulatory metacognition as the process that we use for planning, allocating our mental resources, monitoring our activity and checking that we are doing okay. However, in order to interpret the evidence with respect to how these regulatory processes should be accomplished we need to call upon our metacognitive knowledge. For example, if I am planning how I am going to make decisions about how much time to allocate to each question in an exam script, I will make better decisions if I have a thorough and accurate understanding of which questions I am likely to know the most about, because these are the questions for which I will find it easiest to construct a good answer. The regulatory processes of our metacognition may be referred to as executive functions – but, like all good executives, they need a thorough understanding of what is happening in the activity for which they have executive responsibility. These executive regulatory processes will also need to take into consideration how we are feeling, by connecting with our metasubjective intelligence.

Metacognitive intelligence does not develop evenly and is coupled with our knowledgeable understanding more generally. For example, if I understand more about biology than I do about history my metacognitive intelligence is likely to be more sophisticated when I am using my knowledge of biology than when I am using my knowledge of history.

Several interesting papers report the success that can be achieved when teaching metacognitive skills and knowledge awareness to learners across the ability range (for example see Schraw, 1998). There are also increasingly numerous resources to help teachers build metacognition into their teaching. See, for example, CIEL (n.d.), which also describes the Metacognitive Awareness Inventory (MAI) created by Schraw and Dennison specifically for adult learners to cultivate awareness of metacognitive knowledge and metacognitive regulation.

I find an example from the Brookings Institution (Owen and Vista, 2017) particularly useful for one aspect of metacognition: meaningful self-reflection. It is provided by an Australian history teacher called David Owen. He uses a technique called 'Exit tickets' to help his students to overcome problems and develop self-analytical skills. At the end of each lesson he encourages his students to think about their learning and the challenges they face by completing three 'tickets'. A red ticket asks them what has stopped their learning today, a yellow ticket asks them what questions and new ideas they have considered today and a green ticket asks them to describe what they have understood and learnt. These three tickets help students to think about three key factors of their learning: when they have encountered a challenge, when they have thought differently about something and when they were learning well. The yellow ticket in particular helps students to think about *how* they are learning as opposed to *when* and *what* they are learning. The tickets can be adapted any area of the curriculum and for use with learners of various ages.

Learning to read is such an important activity that unsurprisingly an excellent range of strategies exists for developing metacognitive knowledge and skills that will aid progress. For example, work with college-aged students in the USA by El-Hindi (1996) has illustrated how specific metacognitive strategies taught as an integrated package to students over a six-week period increased students' metacognitive awareness for reading and writing.

The metacognitive strategies that were taught included:

- Planning: students were instructed that they needed to identify a purpose for their reading, activate their prior knowledge, preview the text and make predictions about it.
- Monitoring: students engaged in self-questioning and comprehension to keep track of their success in understanding the text.
- Responding: students were taught to evaluate their understanding, to react to what they had read and to relate the content of their reading to their prior experience.

A second example that focuses on reading can be found at the Cambridge International Education Teaching and Learning team website (CIE Teaching and Learning Team, n.d.) in the shape of 'reciprocal teaching', a research-informed strategy to develop reading comprehension (based on research by Palincsar and Brown in 1984). This involves teachers using four key strategies to support reading comprehension:

- questioning
- clarifying
- summarizing
- predicting.

Students are then asked to take on the role of teacher and teach these strategies to other students – hence the name *reciprocal teaching*. A useful video, 'Students take charge: Reciprocal teaching', by Reading Rockets (2014), illustrates this approach in action with learners.

Our metacognitive intelligence needs not only to know what we know about the world, but also to understand how good we are at constructing knowledge from its component parts. We also need to know in what circumstances particular knowledge can be applied, so we have to be able to index our knowledge contextually. Such contextualization is important if we are to transfer what we have learnt and therefore to know how to apply that knowledge in a different setting or environment from the one in which we acquired it.

AI and Element 4

Metacognitive intelligence is something that is beyond (current) AI. Therefore, in addition to its importance for the development of other elements of our intelligence, metacognitive intelligence is important if we are to outwit AI.

However, AI can be used to help learners increase their metacognitive intelligence. For example, over a series of studies that ran between 2000 and 2007 (Luckin, 2010), colleagues and I used a purpose-built piece of software called the Ecolab to evaluate the extent to which we could support some metacognitive development in children aged 8 to 10 years. We focused in particular on these children's ability to decide the level of difficulty of the activities that they would be able to complete successfully, and on the efficacy and appropriateness with which they selected among a range of context-sensitive help resources. We provided feedback for each child on the effectiveness of their activity difficulty selection and help. We also used this feedback to prompt each child to keep thinking about why they were choosing from among the available options of difficulty and help. The children whose scores increased the most from pre-intervention to post-intervention evaluation were the less able students (Luckin and du Boulay, 2017). This is not an isolated example, and many practical tools have been designed by and for educators to help teach metacognitive skills and knowledge awareness. These studies demonstrate that metacognitive intelligence is not only available to more able learners, as defined by current rather knowledge-focused definitions of 'ability'. Metacognitive intelligence can be developed across learners of all abilities.

Element 5: Metasubjective intelligence

> *Metasubjective knowledge, and skilled metasubjective regulation.* The term *metasubjective* encompasses both our emotional and motivational knowledge and regulatory skills. We need to develop our ability to recognize our emotions and the emotions of others, to regulate our emotions and behaviours with respect to other people and with respect to taking part in a particular activity (our motivation).

Metasubjective intelligence is about the appreciation, understanding and regulation of our unique and individual human subjective experience of the world. Metasubjective knowledge and skilled metasubjective regulation include both emotional and motivational aspects of our intelligence, because emotion and motivation are so closely coupled. Metasubjective intelligence enables us to connect the direct experiences from our senses with our emotions, and with the other elements of our intelligence in a connected whole that is greater than the sum of its parts.

Successful learners can recognize and regulate their emotions with respect to taking part in any activity. The beliefs they hold about their ability to complete a particular activity, their perceived control over that activity and their perceptions about the usefulness of that activity to themselves in the future will all be affected by how they are feeling. These beliefs and self-perceptions will in turn impact upon their motivation and their ability to regulate their feelings towards an activity.

One of the interesting findings in the PISA data concerning collaborative problem-solving, to which I referred earlier, was that learners with a more positive attitude towards collaboration were found to perform better in the collaborative problem-solving assessment. It seems obvious to state that if we feel positive then we are more likely to succeed, but also that the relationship between our learning and our feelings and motivations is complex. Within this element of intelligence I am concerned with our subjective awareness and regulation. In other words, it is not the relationship between someone's motivations and their performance per se that interests me. Rather it is the extent to which that person has an accurate understanding of their emotions and motivations, combined with the skill to regulate the impact of those emotions upon their behaviour.

There are ample examples of methods that can be used to increase student motivation, and a great deal of research evidence that demonstrates whether or not such methods are effective. I gave some examples of this research in Chapter 3, and in particular noted that something as simple as the way in which activity instructions are phrased can have an impact upon students' emotional relationship to that activity, and to the motivation that drives how they complete it. One has only to read about the theory of the 'nudge' in modern behavioural economics to see how easily we can be persuaded, or motivated, towards a particular action (Thaler and Sunstein, 2008).

The thrust of what needs to be done to help develop our students' metasubjective intelligence lies in the provision of teaching approaches that address the needs of individual learners. Many of us have fond memories of a particular teacher at school, and in many instances this is at least partly because that teacher knew how to motivate us to learn. Teachers understand this: they know how important it is to meet the emotional needs of their learners. However, policymaking and curriculum design tends to be a more school-based enterprise. This can result in approaches to education that either enable or disable metasubjective self-belief.

The building of self-belief is not just a case of teaching people to take positive actions and to feel good about themselves as a result. It requires that we teach them to adopt a learning orientation (Crocker and Park, 2004) through which they can see failures as learning opportunities. We need to steer clear of trying to boost learners' belief in themselves merely through praise for what they have just achieved. We must also build belief in our learners that they can further develop their intelligence through effort (Duckworth *et al.*, 2009). This approach might, for example, involve teaching people how to develop good work habits, how to maintain their attention to the task at hand and how to cope emotionally (Boekaerts and Corno, 2005). The TARGET programme (see Ames, 1990, 1992) is a whole-class approach that describes six aspects of classroom structure that teachers can modify to promote their students' self-belief: classrooms adopting this approach have increased the number of students who show evidence of a positive motivation to learn (Duckworth *et al.*, 2009). A second relevant example here is the SEAL programme (Department for Education and Skills, 2005; SEAL Community, n.d.), which was informed by Salovey and Mayer (1990), Goleman (1995) and Dweck (2007). It provides guidance for teachers on how to promote self-belief and instil within learners the belief that they can learn and that they can boost their intelligence.

AI AND ELEMENT 5

Subjectivity is a complex concept that, like the associated concept of consciousness, is something that we know we experience, yet find hard to define or explain. Our consciousness as humans is certainly inextricably linked with our subjective experience, but is it more? I am neither capable of explaining our subjectivity nor our consciousness. I am, however, capable of recognizing that our subjective experience of the world is important to our understanding of it and to our intelligence. I echo Max Tegmark's (2017) sentiments when he suggests that we 'rebrand ourselves as homo sentient'.

Subjective intelligence is beyond current AI, and probably unattainable by future AI, although we cannot be sure. We can, however, be certain that subjective intelligence is something where we humans have power that can humble any AI. This is one excellent reason for making sure that we pay significant attention to developing subjective intelligence through our education systems.

Element 6: Metacontextual intelligence

> Metacontextual knowledge and skills are essential for understanding the way in which our *physical embodiment interacts with our environment, its resources and with other people*. Metacontextual intelligence includes physical intelligence, through which we use our bodies to interact and learn about the world. Metacontextual intelligence is our intellectual bridge to our instinctive mental processes so that we can recognize when they are demanding attention and evaluate if that attention is warranted. Metacontextual intelligence will also help us to recognize when we are biased and when we are succumbing to post hoc rationalization.

The interaction of our mental processes and our physical embodiment with our environment, its resources and the other people who are part of it has a substantial impact upon how and the extent to which we can construct knowledge and understanding. This physical experience is largely a part of our metasubjective intelligence; however, it is also related to the broader context of our learning. It is therefore worthy of attention in its own right. Metacontextual intelligence describes our capacity to understand the relationship that we have with our context and to regulate our interactions in a way that takes the features and demands of our context into account successfully.

If we are to help our students to develop a sophisticated metacontextual intelligence, we need them to do more than develop their emotional and physical intelligence. I have already indicated that all elements of our metalevel intelligences are highly contextualized. For example, our personal epistemology is highly context-specific. Metacontextual intelligence is concerned with our knowledge of the relationship between the other elements of our intelligence and our context. It is about our ability to regulate our intelligent behaviours with respect to our context.

In 2010 I developed and published a design framework called the *Ecology of Resources*, which could be used to help technology developers and educators construct technology or activities using technology that were appropriately context-sensitive. The *Ecology of Resources* draws upon the following learner-centred definition of context:

> A learner is not exposed to multiple contexts, but rather has a single context that is their lived experience of the world, a 'phenomenological gestalt' (Manovich, 2006) that reflects their interactions with multiple people, artefacts and environments. The partial descriptions of the world are offered to a learner through these resources, which act as the hooks for interactions in which action and meaning are built. In this sense, meaning is distributed among these resources. However, it is the manner in which the learner at the centre of their context internalizes their interactions that is the core activity of importance (Luckin, 2010: 18).

To support contextualized learning it is necessary to identify and understand the relationships between the different types of resource with which the learner interacts. In addition it is necessary to explore the manner in which a learner's interactions with these resources is, or might be, constrained. These constraints are identified by the term 'filter'. For example, a learner's access to their teacher is filtered by the school environment's organization and any rules and conventions that apply to it.

The structured process of the *Ecology of Resources* design framework (EoR) is iterative, participatory and has three phases, each of which has several steps:

- *Phase 1:* Create an **ecology of resources model** to identify and organize the potential forms of assistance that can act as resources for learning.
- *Phase 2:* Identify the relationships within and between the resources produced in Phase 1. Identify the extent to which these relationships meet a learner's needs and how they might be optimised with respect to that learner.
- *Phase 3:* Develop the scaffolds and adjustments to support learning: scaffolds help to support learners to achieve success and adjustments

alter the complexity of the activity or task so that the learner is better able to succeed.

An example will help to explain how this works. While working with students and staff at a learning centre in the South East of England for 11–16-year-old learners we used the EoR framework to help them plan a trip to the Royal Observatory, in London. As part of this, we helped students plan their use of technology. For example, the process helped them to identify the various resources at the observatory, and within this they identified that they might attend the planetarium to learn about the Milky Way as part of a particular scheduled show.

The students were able to specify that the show as a resource is filtered by time (show times, length of narrative/visuals about the Milky Way) and by rules (no audio recording or photography allowed, meaning that learners must remember or record what they see in a different way). The ability to make notes about the show is filtered by ambiance. Lack of light in the darkened room acts as a constraining filter for writing. However, if, for example, learners have a mobile phone, backlighting enables note-taking. Listening to the narrator, the presence of the audience and respect for the rules of quiet listening when in company also act as a constraining filter on the learner's ability to use available other people as *in situ* resources. Some of these issues could be addressed in the design process, for example by considering the use of GPS sensors that would 'push' information to learners' mobile phones at various locations; alternatively, for example, the learner could opt to receive additional digital information about specific knowledge concepts via Bluetooth to their mobile phone.

Other researchers have also found this framework useful and have made some valuable additions to the original version. For example, Marcia Lindqvist (2015) used the framework to explore the contextual challenges to the use of digital technologies in Swedish schools. There are, however, few other resources available for teaching metacontextual intelligence and this is an area that will need considerable attention.

AI AND ELEMENT 6

AI has no metacontextual intelligence. It is, however, possible for an AI system to appreciate the microcontext of the information it processes. The microcontext could include, for example, the context of a word or phrase in a news story in terms of the text surrounding it or other texts referring to similar concepts. AI systems that are embodied in robots may have information from sensors that can help them to gain knowledge about their environment, but they have no appreciation of their situatedness in the world beyond these simple inputs, and no way of becoming aware of the rich contexts in which humans move and learn.

As with other elements of human Intelligence, AI can help humans to increase their intelligence. AI can capture and process information about our interactions within the world and in so doing help us to understand the relationships between the different resources with which we interact. For example, we can capture data about our movement, exercise, and diet that can be analysed to help us monitor ourselves in ways that maintain our health. There is then potential to map this on to data about our learning progress to explore how best we maintain the most positive relationships between our physical and intellectual well-being.

Element 7: Perceived self-efficacy

This intelligence element requires an *accurate, evidence-based judgement about our knowledge and understanding, our emotions and motivations and our personal context*. We need to know our ability to succeed in a specific situation and to accomplish tasks both alone and with others. This is the most important element of human intelligence and it is highly connected to the other six.

Perceived self-efficacy is the most important element of human intelligence and it is the key skill that people will need for their future learning and work lives. It requires an accurate, evidence-based judgement about our knowledge and understanding, our emotions and motivations and our personal, subjective experience and context. It pulls together all the other intelligence elements: it is about more than complex, goal-directed behaviour and it is way beyond the powers of AI. The idea of a 'Fitbit for the mind', as suggested in Chapter 5, would be powered by self-efficacy and would provide for the intellect the same faculty that step-recording provides for fitness tracking.

A person's sense of self-efficacy plays a key role in how they tackle tasks and challenges and how they set their goals, both as individuals and as collaborators. It is something that can be taught and mentored and it requires an extremely good knowledge of what one does and does not know, what one is and is not so good at, where one needs help and how to get this help. This self-knowledge is not just about subject-specific knowledge and understanding, but also about well-being, emotional strength and context. It is holistic and currently uniquely human.

Accurate perceived self-efficacy is important for teachers as well as learners. As I reported in Chapter 3, research studies have shown that positive and accurate perceptions of self-efficacy in teachers are related to higher levels of student achievement and motivation. The connection between perceived self-efficacy and the rest of our intelligence is complex and nuanced: each element contributes to our accurate perceived self-efficacy.

This means that we need to know what knowledge is and how we can make evidence-based judgements about our own knowledge and capability (elements 2 and 4). We also need to relate our understanding of our own knowledge and skills to our emotions and motivation so that we can progress with confidence in our capability (elements 4 and 5). To recognize what is required of us as learners, we need to relate the task or activity to what we know and we need to plan and evaluate what we do. And we need to do this with an understanding of the resources available to support us from the environment, from other people, and from tools such as books or the internet, or an AI (elements 2, 4 and 6). If we are to learn with and through others, we need to know and communicate our understanding of the joint activity and interact effectively with other people (elements 3 and 4). All of the elements are inextricably connected into an interwoven whole that is our accurate perceived self-efficacy.

To develop this accurate perceived self-efficacy, we need to connect the development of the algorithmic process that helps us to cultivate sophisticated knowledgeable understanding and skills with the rational metalevel processing that helps us to develop a knowledgeable understanding of ourselves. With respect to Element 1, our academic intelligence, we may have different self-efficacy with respect to different areas of our knowledgeable understanding of the world. In the same way that an orchestra is the co-ordinated performance of multiple elements for the purpose of musical performance, our perceived self-efficacy consists in the co-ordination of our intelligence elements for the purpose of learning. And, in the same way that a particular orchestra may be better at performing a Bach fugue than a Mozart requiem, we as learners may learn more self-efficaciously when it comes to mathematics or problem-solving than we do for drama or physics.

The consequences for education of this need for co-ordination are that we need to look to methods that develop our students across all seven elements of their intelligence. I have already suggested that debating is a good activity to help develop Element 2 meta-knowing, and it can likewise be used to help develop elements 3, 4 and 5 (social, metacognitive and metasubjective intelligence) too. If we look at the 'Exit tickets' activity I suggested for Element 4 (metacognitive intelligence), the red ticket that asked learners what had stopped their learning today could be used as a tool to explore with learners their (Element 5) metasubjective intelligence. The green ticket, which asks learners to describe what they have understood and learned, could be used to develop learners' (Element 2) meta-knowing intelligence by asking them to explain the evidence that justifies their belief that they have understood something.

Perceived self-efficacy should be the primary goal of our education and training.

AI AND ELEMENT 7

The close connection of perceived self-efficacy to the other six intelligence elements makes its cultivation a priority for our use of AI to develop our own abilities. If we design and use AI effectively we can process the increasing amounts of data about each of our interactions in the world to expose the evidence upon which we make judgements about our own knowledge and understanding, and the knowledge and understanding of those we are helping to educate or train. Through the careful, collection, collation and analysis of data, AI will provide us with evidence about each learner's progress, knowledge, skills and interdisciplinary understanding of the world. We can also use AI to analyse and feed back to learners, students, trainees and their educators about how their emotions, motivations, context and subjective experience of the world affect their developing knowledge and understanding. AI systems that can use data to produce detailed analyses of individual behaviours and activities are already being developed, both commercially and in research labs across the world. It is therefore essential that educators are more involved in their design and application so that the development of such systems is informed by experienced educators who understand how people learn.

We must also ensure that the highest ethical principles are applied in determining how AI tracks and analyses individual personal development in detail. AI has the potential to be an enormous force for good in helping everyone to develop a more accurate perception of their self-efficacy and to increase the sophistication and power of their self-efficacy. However, as with all new technologies there will be people who wish to use these aspects of what AI can provide to harm, manipulate and control people in ways that are not beneficial for them. This danger is one of the reasons why we must also ensure that everyone understands enough about AI to protect themselves and their loved ones from harmful applications.

Progression and assessment

At the start of this book, I reflected my concern that we have become obsessed with measuring things. However, there is value in measurement, and in evaluation, if they are tied to a clear specification of what measurement and/or evaluation are aiming to achieve – if they are tied to what success looks like. If I want to become a good professional tennis player I must be clear about how I judge my success, not just on the professional tennis circuit but also for every element of my training. Intelligence is no different. If we want our students, trainees, employees and entrepreneurs to develop their intelligence to the best of their potential, then we need a way to make judgements about the success of each element of their development and the co-ordination of these elements into an interwoven whole.

Education and training should design and use progression models that constantly promote growth across and between all elements of our intelligence. To do this successfully, such models must acknowledge the instinctive mental processing that enables us to automate certain knowledge and skills through practice: the algorithmic process that helps us to develop sophisticated knowledgeable understanding and skills and the rational meta-level processing that helps us to develop a knowledgeable understanding of ourselves. But what might such a progression model look like in practice?

In practical terms, a good progression model on which we can base both teaching and assessment requires:

1. A clear specification of what success looks like – the goal that learners must aim to achieve. This goal must now be one that addresses all the elements of interwoven intelligence. It might best be phrased in terms of the development of accurate perceived self-efficacy. This is not a simple step, but it is one that we must address if we are to break away from education systems that have too much of a focus on teaching humans the things that machines can now do more accurately and faster.
2. Learning activities that break down complex goals into subgoals and subactivities in a manner that will help learners to reach their goal.
3. A mechanism for identifying movement towards a subgoal and a goal.
4. Feedback intended to help learners to move towards their goal and that helps learners know how well they are doing at moving towards their goal. Feedback must be sensitive to the fact that progress may not always be even, and sometimes a step back can be important for achieving an overall goal.

If we simplify step 1, so that it addresses Element 1 (academic knowledge), then this set of steps is at the heart of most AI tutoring systems. The beauty of developing an AI tutor using GOFAI as well as machine learning is that you have to specify subgoals, activities and feedback in considerable detail. The development of progression models like this across all the subject areas we want to teach, and then the building of AI educators to provide individualized tuition for every learner, is technically possible. It is probably also a good idea for helping students to develop their Element 1 intelligence. AI is remarkably consistent, shows no bias and does not get tired. If we design the AI using a sensible combination of old and new AI techniques, we can ensure that our systems' knowledge is always up to date, and we can also ensure that they are able to explain the teaching decisions that they make. The use of AI to teach academic, interdisciplinary knowledgeable understanding and skills would also have the advantage of providing continuous assessment of each individual's progress towards that goal. This would be useful for that individual and the human educator.

The beauty of using AI in this part of teaching is that it means that our human educators can focus their attention upon the remaining six elements of our intelligence and on co-ordinating development across all seven elements of interwoven intelligence. These are the elements that are much harder to automate with AI, the elements that will be essential to our continuing development of sophisticated intelligence that will enable us to outperform AI and robots.

Each of the other six elements of intelligence, beyond our knowledge of the world, need to be the subject of progression-model development through the four steps I identified above. However, this cannot be done in isolation. Progression across the six elements must be integrated, and it must be linked to each learner's progression with their Element 1 knowledge of the world.

AI systems cannot develop the accurate perceived self-efficacy that is needed to drive our education system. They can, however, help us to develop the accurate perceived self-efficacy of our students and of ourselves. The detailed information about learner progress that would be available from the AI tutoring systems developed to support the teaching of knowledge of the world provide the data about individual learners that can also be used to help us understand some aspects of their development of elements of their intelligence beyond Element 1. For example, this data can be analysed to evaluate a learner's perseverance, motivation and aspects of their confidence. This information can then be used by human teachers in their development of the learner's metasubjective intelligence. Data from the AI tutoring systems can also be used to help teachers group students for collaborative problem-solving in ways that are most likely to support their learning, social interaction and the development of their social intelligence. The discussion of signifiers in Chapter 5 illustrates how we might achieve some of this for some social intelligence activities, for example.

The development of progression models for interwoven intelligence, particularly with respect to elements 3 to 6, will be difficult, as was illustrated in Chapter 3. However, the immense amount of research that has already been done for many aspects of epistemic and meta-level cognition can act as a good starting point (Boekaerts, 2006; Flavell, 1979; Hattie *et al.*, 1996; Higgins *et al.*, 2005; King and Kitchener, 1994; Pintrich, 2000b; Ryan and Deci, 2002; Sandoval, 2003; Wiliam, 2012; Frieman, 2014). There are validated tools, such as questionnaires, that can provide some useful interim instruments for identifying goals, activities and feedback (Duncan and McKeachie, 2005; Elshout-Mohr *et al.*, 2003; O'Neil and Abedi, 1996; Pintrich *et al.*, 1993; see also Stelar, n.d.).

Of course, specifying progression beyond Element 1 intelligence will require considerable input from human educators if it is to have any chance of success. These are after all the elements of intelligence that are not available to AI, so it is not surprising that they are not easy to design, evaluate or reproduce. We cannot build AI teachers who can take this workload off human shoulders. We can, however, design AI tools that can help human educators to develop these elements of intelligence much more effectively. These are the tools that I discussed both here and in Chapter 5, when I explored what big data and AI could yield for our increased understanding and identification of our intelligent interactions in the world.

As we design and develop these progression models for all elements of intelligence, we must ensure that we develop responsive assessments, so that we know in a detailed way how learners are improving. We must also ensure that learners are continually supported to develop their own understanding of themselves through these assessments.

In this chapter, I have discussed the implications for education of recognizing a more holistic conceptualization of intelligence, a conceptualization that differentiates humans from AI very clearly. I have indicated that AI can help us to increase Element 1 intelligence of learners through the provision of AI educators. If we do this then we can enable educators to focus on using their uniquely human expertise to develop the other elements of their students' intelligence. In this way, we take best advantage of our human educators' human intelligence. We also ensure that our education system develops learners' intelligence beyond the subject-based knowledge that is easy to automate. There are substantial implications for the way in which we educate and train our educators and trainers.

Educators are immensely skilled and I have no doubt that they are highly able to rise to the challenges of redesigning education systems to accommodate how AI is changing our society. However, they will need support, not least to understand how best to use the data and AI systems that will be increasingly available to them. The first step in any transformation from our current position must focus on these educational practitioners. We must remember that, like most of us, they are also learners at this point in the AI revolution. We must ensure that they are given a voice in the development of the AI systems they will be asked to use. Currently, too many educational technologies, and in particular AI technologies, are developed without sufficient input from the people for whom they are designed. When it comes to education, it is essential that the trained and expert workforce of educators are included as key partners in the design of educational AI systems. It is these educators who understand what is to be taught, how their students learn and what types of system are likely to work in the hustle and bustle of most educational environments.

The need to educate about AI

Before leaving the subject of education, there is one last topic that needs a little attention: education about AI. The key question we need to answer is this: how do we educate people about AI, so that they can benefit from it?

There are three key components that need to be introduced into the curriculum at various stages of education, from early years through to adult education and beyond, if we are to prepare people to gain the greatest benefit from AI. The first is that everyone needs to understand enough about AI to be able to work with AI systems effectively. This part is essential for AI and human intelligence to augment each other and for us to benefit from a symbiotic relationship between the two. For example, people need to understand that AI is as much about the specification of a particular problem and the careful design of a solution as it is about the selection of particular AI methods and technologies to use as part of that problem's solution.

The second key requirement for developing the AI curriculum is that everyone must be involved in a discussion about what AI should and should not be designed to do. Some people need to be trained to tackle the ethics of AI in depth and help decision makers to make appropriate decisions about how AI is going to affect the world. If we ignore the need for education about AI, then we risk failing to empower people to make key decisions about what it should and should not, could and could not, and will and will not be able to do for society.

The third requirement in constructing an AI curriculum is that some people also need to know enough about AI to build the next generation of AI systems. If teachers are to prepare young people for the new world of work, and if teachers are to prime and excite young people to engage with careers designing and building our future AI ecosystems, then someone must train the teachers and trainers and prepare them for their future workplace and its students' needs. This is a role for policymakers, in collaboration with the organizations that govern and manage the various teacher development systems and training protocols across countries. The need for young people to be equipped with knowledge about AI is urgent, and therefore the need for educators to be similarly equipped is critical and imperative.

On a more positive note, the development of AI teaching assistants will provide an opportunity for developing deeper teaching skills and enriching the teaching profession. This deepening of teacher expertise might be at the subject-knowledge level, or could be concerned with developing the requisite skills to support and nurture collaborative problem-solving in our students. It could also result in teachers developing the data science and learning science skills that enable them to gain greater insights from the increasingly available array of data about students' learning.

Any failure to recognize and address the urgent and critical teaching and training requirements precipitated by the advancement and growth of AI is likely to result in a failure to galvanize the prosperity that should accompany the AI revolution.

Summary

Machines can learn, thanks to AI, and they can learn faster and they can recall what they have learnt more accurately than humans can. However, this learning is currently only within the sphere of Element 1 of the interwoven model of intelligence: knowledge about the world. Machines can mimic some of the features of other elements from the interwoven intelligence model, such as emotions, but they feel no emotions, and have no awareness of the subjective experience of any emotions.

Our human ability to learn is the key to 'moving' our intelligence so that we better value and more effectively develop and use all seven elements of intelligence, and in particular our accurate perceived self-efficacy. Societies must fulfil their responsibility to their members by designing and implementing education systems that effectively develop people's interwoven intelligence. To achieve this, education systems need progression models that constantly promote growth across and between all seven intelligence elements. Embracing the AI-augmented world is not simple, however, and while educators are unlikely to be among the early white-collar victims of AI replacement, their lives must and will change forever through it. They will need to teach different material, as well as some of the material they already teach, and they will need to teach differently.

A sophisticated personal epistemology helps people develop sophisticated knowledgeable understanding and skills from their academic studies – and it is beyond the capacity of AI. To extend the initially simple personal epistemologies of our students we need to teach them explicitly about the potential sources of knowledge and the ways in which they can justify that knowledge. We need to help people design and ask good questions that probe the information they are presented with in an appropriate and useful manner. We and they must recognize the contextual nature of their knowledge and its inconsistency.

The final and most important element of human intelligence is perceived self-efficacy. It pulls together all the other intelligence elements and is way beyond the powers of AI. Self-efficacy is important for teachers as well as learners. We can help learners to develop a greater understanding of their own self-efficacy through developing the other six intelligence elements. Self-efficacy needs also to be the focus of specific and explicit teaching. It should be the intelligence that we strive for throughout our lives, within and beyond our formal education and training.

Moving to an intelligence-based curriculum of the sort outlined here will require a transformational change, for which we must plan now. And, as if this were not challenging enough, we also need to teach people about AI, including (and as the highest priority) teaching the teachers and trainers about AI. Education about AI must include several components: teaching people how to work effectively with AI systems; giving people a voice in what AI should and should not be designed to do; and helping some people to build the next generation of AI systems.

AI can help us build our future education systems based on the progression models that include all seven intelligence elements. It is technically straightforward to develop AI to teach academic, interdisciplinary knowledgeable understanding and skills, including the provision of detailed continuous assessment about each individual's progress towards each goal. The use of such systems would free our human educators to focus on the holistic development of their students' interwoven intelligence.

Chapter 7

Social and meta-intelligence: How education can prepare humans for an AI world

In 1996, when John Anderson proposed his definition of intelligence, I don't imagine that his wildest dreams portrayed any glimmer of our current AI. It is unlikely that he could have pictured the resultant dilemma we face, one caused by the fact that we are limiting our appreciation of human intelligence to the terms of the artificial intelligences that we have built. Anderson at that time suggested that

> all that there is to intelligence is the simple accrual and tuning of many small units of knowledge that in total produce complex cognition. The whole is no more than the sum of its parts, but it has a lot of parts (Anderson, 1996: 356).

But the whole *is* more than the sum of its parts, and the 'accrual and tuning' to which Anderson refers is far from simple. We have been all too easily carried away on a wave of technical enthusiasm and have been bamboozled into believing that AI is far more intelligent than it really is. It is now time to take stock, to re-evaluate what we mean by intelligence, to realize the significance and limitations of the 'black box' opacity of machine learning fully. There is cause to be optimistic about our capacity to demand better from our AI technology. This is, for example, manifested in initiatives such as the Explainable AI programme funded by DARPA (XAI; see Chapter 4), and in the calls for intelligible AI (see, for example, House of Lords Artificial Intelligence Committee, 2017). However, we now need to demand more from ourselves. We must focus on the best ways to appreciate and develop the wonder and complexity of the intricate, subjective, emotional and self-knowing thing that human intelligence is. We also need to attend to the relationship between human and artificial intelligences, and to the ways in which we can start to solve some of our biggest challenges through the judicious application of the right blend of the human and the artificial.

Intelligence-based education and training

That AI has gained such traction in the 21st century is largely due to the 'perfect storm' brought about by the availability of large quantities of data, powerful computer processing and large clouds of cheap storage for both raw and processed data that can be accessed from almost anywhere. These three factors – data, computing power and storage – can be combined with sophisticated AI systems that can use the computing power to learn from the data. This perfect storm has enabled us to use AI to build immense 'knowledge' bases that can be sifted and searched with stunning accuracy to pinpoint the minutiae required to diagnose a disease, to process an image, to beat world-champion game players and to help us navigate through our physical and virtual worlds. We can ask our AI who ruled which countries at any particular date in time; we can ask it how to solve an equation and we can ask it to drive a car. The development of AI that can learn faster and more accurately than humans has brought about a situation that requires us to make some dramatic and significant changes to our approach to knowledge within our education and training systems.

Our relationship to knowledge

Knowledge is the lynchpin of many education systems and it remains a key element of our intelligence, but it is merely one element, it is not the whole story. It is the element of our intelligence that is the easiest to automate with AI and we therefore need to revise our relationship to knowledge. We need to consider our knowledge of the world and our interactions with the world *in relation to the other elements of human intelligence*, not as an end in itself. The relationship to knowledge that we build through teaching and learning must now be more sophisticated. As educators, we must more clearly differentiate between information and knowledge. We must develop within our students and trainees the ability to ask good questions, to challenge the evidence we present to them, to understand that knowledge is subjective and contextualized and that we must construct our understanding of the world for ourselves, through social interaction and critical analysis. The development of this healthy scepticism for authority will also encourage people to challenge their AI systems (and their media outlets) and to demand that they are provided with adequate justifications for any information and decisions that such AI systems (or media) assert.

Numeracy and literacy, including data literacy, will of course remain fundamental to all education, as will the basics of AI – not the technical detail of how to code an AI, but the principles and logic upon which such systems are designed. The remaining subject areas are no less important, but the emphasis will need to be on what these subjects are, how they have arisen, why they exist and how to learn them.

In Chapter 6 I described how activities such as debate and collaborative problem-solving can provide powerful ways to help students understand their relationships to knowledge and to hone their ability to challenge and question. To ensure that teachers and trainers have the time to work with their students and trainees to develop these complex skills, we can use AI tutoring systems to help students gain a basic understanding of numeracy and literacy and of the subject knowledge that we wish students to use as exemplars from which they can gain a basic understanding – an understanding that can then be refined through activities such as debate and collaborative problem-solving. This AI can ensure that, as and when appropriate, learners practise and perfect their understanding, and that learners are both appropriately challenged and sufficiently supported.

Our AI can also be turned to good use to analyse the increasingly available data that can be collected about the progress of our learners and trainees as they advance their understanding, as they learn to debate and as they refine their collaborative problem-solving skills. This data can be used to help teachers provide optimal support as and when required and to help learners understand their own ability and progress effectively.

I used the brilliant work of Daniel Kahneman to explain the important relationships between our instinctive thinking and our intellectual and rational thinking. The intellectual mind (System 2) that we cherish so much cannot exist without our instinctive mind (System 1). Our intellectual mind is the home of our algorithmic ability for complex computation, of slow deliberate thinking and of the completion of IQ tests. It is also the home of our uniquely human ability to ignore our biases, to pay attention, maintain our focus and develop our self-control; it helps us to combat our natural intellectual laziness. It is this uniquely human ability that we must nurture through our education and training systems.

We need to work on our relationship to knowledge as much as – possibly even more than – on our knowledge itself. We can do this by developing a sophisticated personal epistemology. It is this that will help us to distinguish between something that can be justified with evidence and something that is simply an opinion. For example, the statement 'Donald J. Trump was inaugurated as president of the United States of America in January 2017' is backed up by lots of solid evidence and we can believe that this statement is justifiably true. In contrast, the statement 'there is no scientific evidence that climate change is real' is merely an opinion that some people believe to be true. There is evidence both for and against this opinion; we need to be able to weigh it up and decide for ourselves whether we are going to share it or not. Our ability to differentiate between justifiable truth, opinion and fiction is a vital element of our human intelligence. And it is an element that is all too often ignored.

Education must help learners to appreciate that their beliefs about the world at any moment in time are the result of their experiences in the world: these beliefs are contextualized. Acknowledging that knowledge and belief are contextualized is vital to our appreciation that our beliefs can be changed without our conscious realization. In turn, knowing that we can be unaware that our beliefs have changed is important for our knowledge of ourselves. It should motivate us to develop better abilities for accurate reconstruction of our experiences and reduce our propensity to take the easy path of post hoc rationalization. We need to embrace our human fallibility if we are to develop the sophisticated intelligence that the challenges of our world now demand from us.

Our relationship to others

Social intelligence is the basis of thought, for how we progress in the world and for how we perceive intelligence. Social intelligence is beyond the capability of AI and increasingly at a premium as more AI is absorbed into the workplace. Social interaction is also the foundation of communal intelligence, another factor that differentiates human and artificial intelligence. There is also a meta-aspect to social intelligence through which we can develop an awareness of, and the ability to regulate, our own social interactions.

We know that talking and social interaction are vital components in the development of our children (Wood, 1990): even at a very young age babies benefit from parents and carers who talk to them (Brown, 1973; Sylva *et al.*, 2010). We encourage reading to children long before they are capable of decoding the words for themselves, because we know it will bring intellectual benefits (Elkin, 2014). However, through much of their subsequent education our children will be evaluated by means of assessments of their individual performance. There are a few examples of assessment within formal education that take into account the students' ability to interact socially, to learn with and through others, and yet so much of the workplace is concerned with team enterprise. Until now, this was defendable because we, as educators, could point to the need for students to be able to evidence their understanding of the knowledge-based curriculum. We needed them to be well grounded in an understanding of a broad curriculum. However, now that we have machines that can absorb this knowledge base, we must consider how better to evaluate our students' social intelligence, their relationship to others and their relationships to their knowledge of the world.

The OECD PISA 2015 evaluation (published in 2017) of collaborative problem-solving to which I referred in Chapter 6 is an example of one possible way forward. This assessment was done via a computer, with the computer playing the part of the student's collaborator. There is no reason why we should not use similar principles to design continuous formative assessments of the way in which our students solve problems both with other human collaborators and with artificially intelligent collaborators. We are also now in a position to use AI to evaluate the extent to which students can achieve greater performance in applying their knowledge to solve problems, both alone and with others, across a wide range of disciplinary and interdisciplinary problem sets (see, for example, Aleven *et al.*, 2009; Koedinger *et al.*, 2012; Luckin, 2017a; Luckin *et al.*, 2016).

We can use AI to help us to both support and assess our students as they develop their academic and their social intelligence. We do, however, need to invest in the development of these AI systems as a matter of urgency. We must also take great care to ensure these systems give significant credit to students who persevere and overcome difficulties, so that we recognize these vital qualities as well as the acquisition of disciplinary and interdisciplinary skill and knowledge.

Our relationship to ourselves

Meta-intelligence is essential to increasing the sophistication of our intelligence. Our meta-intelligence includes four elements:

- *Metacognition*: our knowledge and control of our own cognitive processes;
- *Meta-emotion*: our awareness of how we feel and how this impacts upon what we know and how we learn;
- *Metacontextual awareness*: our physical and mental abilities and awareness of our interactions with the world, including our social interactions;
- *Accurate perceived self-efficacy*.

I have discussed each of these elements in some detail in Chapter 6.

The elements of our meta-intelligence are all interrelated in complex ways to each other and to our knowledge, our personal epistemology and our social intelligence. For example, our motivation to learn is closely intertwined with our metacognition, and vice versa. Our meta-intelligence is also concerned with our physical presence in the world and our awareness of it: our metacontextual intelligence. This in turn impacts upon our beliefs about our ability and power, for example. The all-important final element of meta-intelligence is perceived self-efficacy. People with higher levels of perceived self-efficacy perform better, waste less time and effort, and suffer less dissatisfaction. An accurate perceived self-efficacy, based on accurate judgements about what we know, is a key ability for learning and will be so to an increasing extent. It will be *the* most important ability for our future lifelong learning. It is also something that is unavailable to AI.

As with both academic and social intelligence, solving the challenge of assessing meta-intelligence will be crucial. It is clear that assessment systems drive the nature of education systems across the globe (see, for example, Black and Wiliam, 1998). Therefore, we need to devise acceptable, rigorous tools to assess the development of our students' meta-intelligences. This is possible. We can probe our students to make explicit their knowledge of their own ability, their appreciation of their capability, their understanding of their physical presence within the world and their awareness and comprehension of their own emotions with respect to their learning. We can use AI to track the progress of the results of this probing: we can compare what each student makes explicit about their self-understanding to the evidence from our tracking of their development of academic and social intelligence. We can then use this comparative information to scaffold learners to develop more sophisticated meta-intelligence.

As with academic and social intelligence, we need to invest in the development of the AI systems to support and evaluate our students' meta-intelligence, and there are numerous existing systems that can act as starting points (see, for example, Arroyo *et al.*, 2009; Baker *et al.*, 2007; Bull *et al.*, 2003; D'Mello *et al.*, 2007; Dragon *et al.*, 2008; Graesser *et al.*, 2008; Johnson, 2007; Kapoor *et al.*, 2007; Kim, 2007; Kleinsmith *et al.*, 2005; Leelawong and Biswas, 2008; McQuiggan and Lester, 2006; Picard, 2000; Soller and Lesgold, 2003).

AI in education for all

The benefits of such AI approaches to support and assessment are not limited to more able learners; there are ample examples of AI systems that can support disadvantaged learners and those with special needs. For example, the use of natural language processing to enable the development of voice-activated interfaces can be helpful for students with physical disabilities that restrict their use of other input devices, such as keyboards. The combination of artificial intelligence and other technologies such as virtual and augmented reality can help students with physical and learning disabilities to engage with virtual environments and take part in activities that would be impossible for them in the real world. AI might be used simply to enhance the virtual world, giving it the ability to interact with and respond to the user's actions in ways that feel more natural. Or AI might provide ongoing intelligent support and guidance to ensure that the learner engages properly with the intended learning objectives without becoming confused or overwhelmed.

AI is currently being used with students diagnosed with attention deficit hyperactivity disorder (ADHD) in work being done at Athabasca University in Canada. The long-term goal of this work is to develop an AIED (artificial intelligence for education – otherwise, learning analytics) system with several features:

- It detects ADHD earlier than current models.
- It improves the quality of diagnosis of ADHD.
- It educates instructors about methods that are effective for teaching students with ADHD.
- It formatively and observationally measures the competency improvements and challenges experienced by students with ADHD.
- It engages with and encourages students with ADHD to study in an environment filled with anthropomorphic pedagogical agents (Mitchnick *et al.*, 2017).

A range of interesting work has been conducted to help people who have autism spectrum disorder. This has included, for example, using AI pedagogical agents and personalized learning (Mohamad *et al.*, 2004). Systems that leverage so-called big data (large volumes of data) to help individual learners can also address special needs requirements: see, for example, work with the nStudy software system at Simon Fraser University (EdPsychLab, n.d.). Separately, the ECHOES project developed at UCL created a technology-enhanced learning environment for typically developing children and children on the autism spectrum. This work used existing technologies such as interactive whiteboards, gesture- and gaze-tracking and intelligent context-sensitive interfaces to create an interactive multimodal environment that adapted to the needs of specific individual children (see Rajendran *et al.*, 2013 and Avramides *et al.*, 2010).

The promise of AI is beyond most people's understanding and its effects are and will continue to be profound. It will change our world for ever and each of our lives will be subject to the ways in which AI is integrated into our world. Without question, some of the tasks that we previously thought of as intelligent tasks are moving from human to machine and we must prepare for some of our intellectual activity to be taken on by AI. This requires that we monitor our own intelligence and that we make sure we are really using it and keeping it up to date. We must all adapt to change thoughtfully, and offload intelligent activity to AI carefully so that we maintain the integrity of our human intelligence. We must resist the temptation to languish in outdated definitions of intelligence. Rather we must learn to enjoy developing our intelligence, accepting that we will never be intelligent enough and that we must always keep learning. The human dilemma precipitated by AI is both beautiful and dangerous. We have created AI technology in our own image of intelligence, and in the process we have diminished our valuation of our own intelligence. But we can use AI to help us develop our human intelligence beyond the ways in which our AI technology can develop its own intelligence.

It is possible to collect data about our every word, movement and action. But we need to be cautious about how much, when and where we collect this data in order to respect people's privacy and to behave ethically. We need people to provide their consent for this data collection and that consent must be informed: the consenter must understand enough about data and AI to be able to know what they are consenting to. Crucially, we need to know the 'right' questions to ask of the data. Only then can we design the AI to process our data most usefully. We can use our AI technology to look for patterns in this data that represent the development of our human intelligence repertoire, to tell us more about ourselves and our intellectual development.

Computer science and AI in the curriculum

It is tempting to address the impact of artificial intelligence in the workplace and within education from the perspective of computer science. This somewhat technocentric perspective is understandable, because it is after all computer science that has built the AI systems we use today: it is therefore understandable that we would look to disciplines such as computer science to help us as we deal with an increasing number of such systems. It is certainly true that we need to engage a more diverse population in acquiring the skills to design and develop the future of our artificial intelligences. However, while this is important it is applicable only to a minority of the population, whereas understanding enough about AI to use it effectively and to make sound decisions about whether or not to allow it into our lives is something that everyone needs to understand. I therefore urge that we adopt a more human-centred approach to education.

I have previously identified two key dimensions that need to be addressed in this approach (Luckin, 2017):

- How can AI improve education and help us to address some of the big challenges we face?
- How do we educate people about AI so that they can benefit from it?

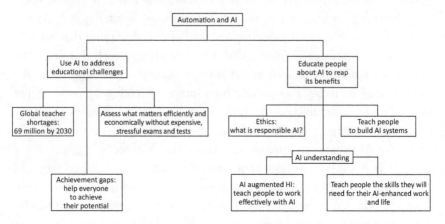

Figure 7.1: The AI and education knowledge tree with its two dimensions (Luckin, 2017b: 111)

I have already said a great deal in this book about the first of these dimensions and the need for the thoughtful design of AI approaches to educational challenges. I have stressed that this enterprise must start with a thorough exploration and specification of the educational problem to be tackled, not with the technology. Only when a well-designed solution to a well-understood educational challenge exists can we start to consider what role AI can best play in that solution and what type of AI technology or technique is best suited to achieving a solution.

There are three key parts to the second dimension of the AI and education tree in Figure 7.1, each of which needs to be introduced into the curriculum at several education stages, from early years to adult education, to prepare people to reap the greatest benefits from AI. One of the key aspects to this second dimension concerns technical knowledge, and ensuring that we have enough diversity in the population who will build the AI systems of the future. We need to bear in mind, however, that much of this will be about clever design and comparatively less will be about writing computer code. To some extent at least our future AI systems will be able to code parts of themselves.

The two much larger parts of this second dimension are concerned with what many more people will need to understand. First, everyone, including those who are currently out of work and outside any educational or training system, will need to understand enough about what AI is to use it effectively. This means that we all need to understand the principles of what AI means, what it can and cannot achieve, what we can and should expect from our AI and what AI is not capable of achieving. It is important that we do not succumb to the notion that this understanding of the basic principles of AI is beyond the capability of society at large. We need to find ways to explain it to people to ensure that they are able to make informed decisions about how they use AI in their lives.

Second, we need to ensure that enough people understand the subtler and more nuanced implications of what AI can and cannot achieve either directly or indirectly, in order to ensure that the appropriate ethical and regulatory mechanisms are in place. History is strewn with examples demonstrating that, left to our own devices, we do not always invariably act in a manner that benefits societies as a whole rather than specific populations.

The three components of this second dimension cannot be dealt with discretely: they are interconnected and must inform each other. For example, the minority of people who develop the AI systems of the future need to communicate with those who develop the regulatory frameworks to ensure that the implications of our AI systems are fully understood and encompassed. In turn those who work with the ethical regulatory requirements must ensure that the manner in which members of society are educated and engaged in understanding their AI systems is sufficient and fit for purpose. Above all we must prioritize the education and training of our educators and trainers. The vast majority currently have little or no understanding of AI, its implications and how they must now change their practice to both encompass its use and build within their students an appropriate understanding of AI as well as a sophisticated level of intelligence across all seven elements I have described in this book. Any failure to recognize and address the urgent and critical educator training requirements implicit in societies' adoption of AI is likely to result in increased disadvantage, poor productivity and increased vulnerability.

Imagination and creativity

It would be inappropriate to finish a book about intelligence without some discussion of creativity and imagination. They are after all essential human capacities and, as I noted in Chapter 1, Einstein is believed to have equated intelligence with imagination. In Chapter 6, I discussed creativity and imagination within the context of 21st century skills and innovation. I noted that creativity can be assisted through large bodies of knowledge that have been securely committed to memory. Creativity and imagination enable us to express our thoughts, feelings and desires, and they underpin scientific and technological development too. However, I do not see creativity and imagination as a separate sort of intelligence. I see them as the result of the development of all seven elements of our human intelligence.

Creativity and imagination can be nurtured by education, although systems that focus primarily on knowledge acquisition, where there is an emphasis on testing and examinations, can hamper learners' capacity to be imaginative and creative. There are some excellent books about how imagination and creativity can be nurtured (see, for example, Cochrane and Cockett, 2007; Cochrane, 2012; Hannon *et al.*, 2013; Lucas *et al.*, 2013; QCA, 2004; Sefton-Green *et al.*, 2011; Sorrel *et al.*, 2014; Sternberg, 1999). Some of the key aspects of behaviour that have been identified as being associated with creativity include being curious, questioning, and being willing to explore and challenge one's assumptions. Persistence is also important, as is being confident enough to be different and capable of coping with a degree of uncertainty, as well as having the ability to focus and direct one's attention.

Creativity and imagination are also sought by AI system designers, but with limited success. There have been some interesting recent developments, with AI used to create a movie trailer for 20th Century Fox (Smith, 2016), for example, as well as successes with art (Roach, 2018) and music (Hutson, 2017). Margaret Boden (1990, 1998) believes that there is still much for us to learn about human creativity and that AI can help us to understand more about our own creativity. Boden draws a useful distinction between *exploratory* and *transformational* creativity: the former can be thought of as finding something new from within an existing space of possibilities, and accounts for the vast majority of what human creativity produces, whereas the latter requires a paradigm shift to a new conceptual space. Machine learning using neural network systems can identify a novel item, a random combination of musical notes, for example, or a mix of colours and shapes. This will fall within the exploratory form of creativity.

Art and drama

Recent decades have seen increasing amounts of content in many school, college and university curricula. Concerns have been raised about the extent to which subjects such as art and drama are being squeezed out by cost-cutting and/or in order to make way for other academic subject areas (see, for example, Johnes, 2017; Alexander, 2017). Throughout this book I have stressed the need for a more sophisticated education system that ensures that our students are even smarter than ever before. It is much harder to develop a sophisticated personal epistemology that enables one to construct an evidence-based understanding of a complex and contested subject than it is to learn and memorize features of that subject for future communication and application. It is often much easier to solve a problem alone, if that problem is tractable enough for one person to tackle, than to work with others to solve a more unwieldy and complicated problem. The intelligence-based approach that I suggest in this book is not an easy option. It does, however, provide an opportunity for subjects such as art and drama to find their way back into the curriculum with greater force. The intelligence-based approach depends far less on absorbing large amounts of academic information into memory, and far more on understanding how to construct understanding and commit knowledge to memory, when it is appropriate to do this, why it is appropriate to do this and for what purpose. A carefully designed intelligence-based approach should allow more space for subjects like art and drama and it should engage these subjects as tools to develop the multiple elements of human intelligence.

The future of education

AI is taking over a great deal of what has previously been viewed as the human domain. As a result, the evidence that we need to change the way we view intelligence and the way we design our education systems is increasingly compelling. We need to act on this evidence and use our human ingenuity to re-imagine our education systems to enable us to remain the smartest intelligence on the planet.

Some of the educational changes that are now essential will be easier to deliver than others. For example, we know that humans can excel at social interaction and that their abilities can be developed through education and training – something that is difficult, probably impossible, for AI. This requires that educators are trained to integrate social interaction effectively in formal and informal education.

Designing progression models to underpin teaching beyond academic knowledge will require considerable human effort. However, there is a significant body of existing research that can help. This research can help us to specify the development of metacognitive intelligence across learners of all abilities, and to grasp how metacontextual intelligence can be improved by helping people to search for and use the learning resources available within their personal contexts. And we already know some of the ways in which we can pull together the elements of human intelligence to help people develop an accurate perceived self-efficacy. We are perfectly capable of designing the progression models we need. We just need to put our minds to the task. We know how to define clear goals and subgoals, identify successful movement towards them, provide sensitive feedback to help learners to move towards them, and help learners know how well they are doing at moving towards them. These are the components that we must now integrate to develop the next-generation progression models our education systems require.

It is our rich and sophisticated human intelligence that makes us perfectly capable of developing the progression models to underpin all of the seven intelligence elements I have outlined in this book. And we are also perfectly capable of developing the AI to help us build our future education systems based on these progression models. Our technical accomplishments to date make it straightforward to develop AI to teach academic, interdisciplinary knowledgeable understanding and skills, including the provision of continuous assessment about each individual's progress towards each goal. Once in place, these AI systems will support our human educators to focus on the remaining elements of our intelligence: namely our social and meta-intelligence.

I cannot conclude this book without sounding a note of caution. We live in times of financial stricture; there is therefore a risk that politicians, managers and decision-makers will be tempted by the inevitable enticements of a growing band of technology companies to believe that education and training can manage with fewer teachers and trainers, and that artificially intelligent tutors can be employed instead of human educators. This would be both incorrect and disastrous. It is true that artificially intelligent tutors can help us to address teacher recruitment and retention problems, but that is only because these AI systems can help to support teachers and to enable them to address the increasing needs of their students: needs that require a human touch. AI can enrich the teaching profession and it can enrich the experiences of our learners and our trainees. It is essential that educators engage in conversations about how AI can best be used in education to ensure that the blend of human and artificial improves the lives of both teachers and learners, as well as all the other educational stakeholders. AI offers an opportunity for educational equality, for improving the education of everyone. We can use AI to tailor educational resources, to help human teachers target their support, to connect learners to teachers across the globe and to engage disabled people, through intelligent interfaces and mixed realities that enable them to experience the world in new and previously impossible ways. However, while I have tremendous faith in human compassion and our desire for good, the evidence of our failure to address social mobility in many parts of the world acts as a stark reminder that we can be somewhat self-centred and blinkered when it comes to our education systems. There is an all too real possibility of a dystopian future in which the poorer and less advantaged of the world are provided with artificially intelligent education technology to tutor them in the basics of a designated curriculum, along with childminders and bouncers to ensure that the requisite time is spent on task and that they are kept safe while the parents and carers work. The more privileged of society would receive a much richer, human-led educational experience where the AI acts as the educator's assistant and as a tool enabling them to focus on a rich curriculum that addresses all elements of their students' intelligence. We must recognize the real possibility of increased social immobility and guard against it.

I have two hopes for this book: that it will raise awareness about the problems of undervaluing our own human intelligence, and that it will act as a call to arms to engage our human intelligence in finding better ways to recognize and develop this human intelligence way beyond the power and potential of AI.

I end on a positive note, because there is in my perception an overwhelming body of evidence that we humans have the creative, resourceful intelligence to address the educational and therefore social challenge we now face. Over the past two decades we have used our technology to re-invent many human activities, from shopping to travel and social networking. It is now time to turn our creative attention to re-inventing the way we help people to learn: the way we help them to develop their human intelligence. We will not necessarily come up with the best solution the first time we try, but this should not deter us, we should merely view our inevitable failures as stepping stones to future success. eBay, Airbnb and Facebook were preceded by the likes of bulletin boards, Craigslist and Friends Reunited. Some of these forerunners are still in operation, others have fallen by the wayside. Education is of course much more complex than buying baked beans, booking a flight or liking a friend's photo. But this just means that we have to apply every element of our intelligence to re-imagine a world wherein everyone learns to develop all elements of their human intelligence.

References

ABC (2018) *The AI Race*. The Australian Broadcasting Commission. Online. www.abc.net.au/tv/programs/ai-race/ (accessed 13 February 2018).

'AI' (2005) *Oxford Dictionary of English*. Oxford: Oxford University of Press.

AlphaBeta (2017) 'The Automation Advantage: How Australia can seize a $2 trillion opportunity from automation and create millions of safer, more meaningful and more valuable jobs'. Online. www.alphabeta.com/wp-content/uploads/2017/08/The-Automation-Advantage.pdf (accessed 13 February 2018).

Alelo (2018) www.alelo.com/ (accessed 4 April 2018).

Aleven, V., McLaren, B.M., Sewall, J. and Koedinger, K.R. (2009) 'A new paradigm for intelligent tutoring systems: example-tracing tutors'. *International Journal of Artificial Intelligence in Education*, 19 (2), 105–54.

Alexander, R. (2017) 'The arts in schools: Making the case, heeding the evidence'. Paper presented at a conference on Intercultural Dimensions of Cultural Education, University of Chester, 13 July 2017. Online. www.robinalexander.org.uk/wp-content/uploads/2017/07/Alexander_Curious_Minds_July17.pdf (accessed 9 May 2018).

American Psychological Association (1996) 'Intelligence: Knowns and unknowns'. *American Psychologist*, 51 (2), 77–101. Online. http://differentialclub.wdfiles.com/local--files/definitions-structure-and-measurement/Intelligence-Knowns-and-unknowns.pdf (accessed 9 February 2018).

Ames, C. (1990) 'Motivation: What teachers need to know'. *Teachers College Record*, 91 (3), 409–21.

Ames, C. (1992) 'Classrooms: Goals, structures and student motivation'. *Journal of Educational Psychology*, 84 (3), 261–71.

Anderson, J. (1996) 'ACT: A simple theory of complex cognition'. *American Psychologist*, 51 (4), 355–65.

Anderson, J.R., Reder, L.M. and Simon, H.A. (1995) 'Applications and misapplications of cognitive psychology to mathematics education'. Online. http://act-r.psy.cmu.edu/papers/misapplied.html (accessed 9 May 2018).

Arroyo, I., Cooper, D.G., Burleson, W., Woolf, B.P., Muldner, K. and Christopherson, R. (2009) 'Emotion sensors go to school'. In Dimitrova, V., Mizoguchi, R., du Boulay, B. and Grasser, A. (eds) *Artificial Intelligence in Education. Building Learning Systems that Care: from Knowledge Representation to Affective Modelling*. Frontiers in Artificial Intelligence and Applications vol. 200. Amsterdam: IOS Press, 17–24.

Atwell, N. (2007) *The Reading Zone: How to help kids become skilled, passionate, habitual, critical readers*. New York: Scholastic.

Avramides, K. (2009) 'An Investigation into Students' Understanding of Knowledge Justification in Psychology Using a Software Tool: Theory and Method in the Study of Epistemic Cognition'. Ph.D. diss., University of Sussex.

Avramides, K., Bernardini, S., Chen, J., Frauenberger, C., Foster, M.E., Lemon, O. and Porayska-Pomsta, K. (2010) 'ECHOES: Technology-enhanced learning for exploring and improving social interaction skills'. Poster presented at the fourth International Conference on Cognitive Systems (CogSys 2010), held in Zurich, 27–28 January. Online. www.cogsys2010.ethz.ch/doc/cogsys2010_proceedings/cogsys2010_0141.pdf (accessed 9 May 2018).

Baines, E., Blatchford, P. and Kutnick, P. (2003) 'Changes in grouping practice over primary and secondary school'. *International Journal of Educational Research*, 39 (1), 9–34.

Baines, E., Blatchford, P. and Kutnick, P.J. (eds) (2016) *Promoting Effective Group Work in the Primary Classroom: A handbook for teachers and practitioners*. 2nd ed. Abingdon and New York: Routledge.

Baker, R.S.J., Rodrigo, M.M.T. and Xolocotzin, U.E. (2007) 'The dynamics of affective transitions in simulation problem-solving environments'. In Paiva, A., Prada, R. and Picard, R.W. (eds) *ACII '07 Proceedings of the 2nd International Conference on Affective Computing and Intelligent Interaction*, held in Lisbon, Portugal, 12–14 September 2007. *Lecture Notes in Computer Science*, 4738. Berlin and Heidelberg: Springer, 666–77.

Balaam, M. (2009) 'Exploring the Emotional Experiences of High School Students with a Subtle Stone Technology'. D.Phil. diss., University of Sussex.

Bandura, A. (1982) 'Self-efficacy mechanism in human agency'. *American Psychologist*, 37 (2), 122–47.

Baxter Magolda, M.B. (1992) *Knowing and Reasoning in College: Gender-related patterns in students' intellectual development*. San Francisco: Jossey Bass.

Baxter Magolda, M.B. (2004) 'Evolution of a constructivist conceptualization of epistemological reflection'. *Educational Psychologist*, 39 (1), 31 -42.

Baxter Magolda, M.B. and Porterfield, W.D. (1985) 'A new approach to assess intellectual development on the Perry scheme'. *Journal of College Student Personnel*, 26 (4), 343–51.

Baxter Magolda, M.B. and Porterfield, W.D. (1988) *Assessing Intellectual Development: The link between theory and practice*. Alexandria, VA: American College Personnel Association.

Beane, J. (1997) *Curriculum Integration: Designing the core of democratic education*. New York: Teachers College Press.

Belenky, M., Clichy, B., Goldberger, N. and Tarule, J. (1986) *Women's Ways of Knowing*. New York: Basic Books.

Bergin, D.A., Ford, M.E. and Hess, R.D. (1993) 'Patterns of motivation and social behaviour associated with microcomputer use of young children'. *Journal of Educational Psychology*, 85 (3), 437–45.

Black, P. and Wiliam, D. (1998) 'Assessment and classroom learning'. *Assessment in Education: Principles, Policy and Practice*, 5 (1), 7–74.

Blatchford, P., Baines, E., Rubie-Davies, C., Bassett, P. and Chowne, A. (2006) 'The effect of a new approach to group-work on pupil–pupil and teacher–pupil interactions'. *Journal of Educational Psychology*, 98, 750–65.

Boekaerts, M. (2006) 'Self-regulation and effort investment'. In Renninger, K.A. and Siegel, I.E. (eds) *Handbook of Child Psychology* vol. 4: *Child Psychology in Practice*. 6th ed. New York: John Wiley and Sons, 345–77.

Boden, M.A. (1980) *Jean Piaget*. New York: Viking Press.

References

Boden, M.A. (1990) *The Creative Mind: Myths and mechanisms*. London: Weidenfeld and Nicholson.

Boden, M.A. (1998) 'Creativity and artificial intelligence'. *Journal of Artificial Intelligence*, 103 (1–2), 247–56.

Boden, M.A. (2016) *AI: Its nature and future*. Oxford: Oxford University Press.

Boekaerts, M. (2003) 'Towards a model that integrates motivation, affect and learning'. *British Journal of Educational Psychology* Monograph Series II (2) – Development and Motivation, 1 (1), 173–89.

Boekaerts, M. and Corno, L. (2005) 'Self-regulation in the classroom: A perspective on assessment and intervention'. *Applied Psychology*, 54, 267–99.

Boomer, G., Lester, N., Onore, C. and Cook, J. (eds) (1992) *Negotiating the Curriculum: Educating for the 21st century*. London: Falmer.

Brown, J.S., Collins, A. and Duguid, P. (1989) 'Situated cognition and the culture of learning'. *Educational Researcher*, 18 (1), 32–42.

Brown, P.C., Roediger III, H.L. and McDaniel, M.A. (2014) *Make it Stick: The science of successful learning*. Cambridge, MA: The Belknap Press of Harvard University.

Brown, R. (1973) *A First Language: The early stages*. Cambridge, MA: Harvard University Press.

Bruner, J. (1996) *The Culture of Education*. Cambridge, MA: Harvard University Press.

Buehl, M.M. and Alexander, P.A. (2006) 'Examining the dual nature of epistemological beliefs'. *International Journal of Educational Research*, 45, 28–42.

Bull, S., Greer, J. and McCalla, G. (2003) 'The caring personal agent'. *International Journal of Artificial Intelligence in Education*, 13 (1), 21–34.

Cambridge Assessment (n.d.) 'Getting started with metacognition'. Online. https://cambridge-community.org.uk/professional-development/gswmeta/index.html (accessed 4 April 2018).

Cambridge Union (2018) 'History of the Union'. Online. https://cus.org//about/history-union (accessed 4 April 2018).

Carnegie Learning (n.d.) Online. www.carnegielearning.com/ (accessed 4 April 2018).

Center for Theory of Change (2017) 'What is theory of change?' Online. www.theoryofchange.org/what-is-theory-of-change/ (accessed 4 April 2018).

Century Tech (2018) www.century.tech/ (accessed 4 April 2018).

Chandramohan, B. and Fallows, S.J. (eds) (2009) *Interdisciplinary Learning and Teaching in Higher Education: Theory and practice*. New York: Routledge.

Christodoulou, D. (2014) *Seven Myths About Education*. London: Routledge.

CIEL (n.d.) 'Ten metacognitive teaching strategies'. Vancouver Island University. Online. https://ciel.viu.ca/teaching-learning-pedagogy/designing-your-course/how-learning-works/ten-metacognitive-teaching-strategies (accessed 9 May 2018).

CIE Teaching and Learning Team (n.d.) 'Getting started with metacognition'. Cambridge Assessment International Education. Online. https://cambridge-community.org.uk/professional-development/gswmeta/index.html (accessed 9 May 2018).

Cochrane, P. (2012) 'Being creative about nurturing creativity'. *Curriculum Briefing*, 10 (2), 3–8.

Cochrane, P. and Cockett, M. (2007) *Building a Creative School: A dynamic approach to school development*. Stoke on Trent/Sterling: Trentham Books.

Cohen, E.G. (1994) 'Restructuring the classroom: Conditions for productive small groups'. *Review of Educational Research*, 64 (1), 1–35.

Copeland, B.J. (2000) 'What is artificial intelligence?' AlanTuring.net. Online. www.alanturing.net/turing_archive/pages/reference%20articles/what%20is%20 ai.html (accessed 9 May 2018).

Crocker, J. and Park, L. (2004) 'Reaping the benefits of pursuing self-esteem without the costs? Reply to DuBois and Flay (2004), Sheldon (2004), and Pyszczynski and Cox (2004)'. *Psychological Bulletin*, 130 (3), 430–34.

Cukurova, M., Luckin, R. and Baines, E. (2018) 'The significance of context for the emergence and implementation of research evidence: the case of collaborative problem-solving'. *Oxford Review of Education*, 44 (3), 322–37. DOI: 10.1080/03054985.2017.1389713

D'Mello, S., Picard, R.W. and Graesser, A. (2007) 'Toward an affect-sensitive AutoTutor'. *IEEE Intelligent Systems*, 22 (4), 53–61.

D'Souza, C. (2013) 'Debating: a catalyst to enhance learning skills and competencies'. *Education + Training*, 55 (6), 538–49. Online. https://doi. org/10.1108/ET-10-2011-0097 (accessed 30 April 2018).

Damon, W. and Phelps, E. (1989) 'Strategic uses of peer learning in children's education'. In Berndt, T.J. and Ladd, G.W. (eds) *Peer Relationships in Child Development*. New York: Wiley, 135–57.

de Kerckhove, D. and Tursi, A. (2009) 'The life of space'. *Architectural Design*, 79 (1), 48–53.

DeBacker, T.K. Crowson, H.M., Beesley, A.D., Thoma, S.J. and Hestevold, N. (2008) 'The challenges of measuring epistemic beliefs: an analysis of three self-report instruments'. *Journal of Experimental Education*, 76 (3), 281–312.

Debate Mate (2018) 'Debate Mate'. Online. https://debatemate.org/ (accessed 30 April 2018).

Department for Education (2014) 'National curriculum in England: English programmes of study'. Online. www.gov.uk/government/publications/national-curriculum-in-england-english-programmes-of-study/national-curriculum-in-england-english-programmes-of-study (accessed 4 April 2018).

Department for Education and Skills (2005) 'Social and emotional aspects of learning: Improving behaviour, improving learning'. London: Department for Education and Skills. Online. http://webarchive.nationalarchives. gov.uk/20110812101121/http://nsonline.org.uk/node/87009 (accessed 9 April 2018).

Digital, Culture, Media and Sport Committee (n.d.) 'Fake news'. Online. www. parliament.uk/business/committees/committees-a-z/commons-select/digital-culture-media-and-sport-committee/inquiries/parliament-2017/fake-news-17-19/ (accessed 11 February 2018).

Dourish, P. (2001) *Where the Action is: The foundations of embodied interaction*. Cambridge: MIT Press.

References

Dragon, T., Arroyo, I., Woolf, B.P., Burleson, W., Kaliouby, R. and Eydgahi, H. (2008) 'Viewing student affect and learning through classroom observation and physical sensors'. In Woolf, B.P., Aïmeur, E., Nkambou, R. and Lajoie, S.L. (eds) *Intelligent Tutoring Systems*. Proceedings of the ninth International Intelligent Tutoring Systems Conference, ITS 2008, held in Montreal, Canada, 23–27 June 2008. Guildford: Springer, 29–39.

du Boulay, B., Avramides, K., Luckin, R., Martínez-Mirón, E., Méndez, G.R. and Carr, A. (2010) 'Towards systems that care: A conceptual framework based on motivation, metacognition and affect'. *International Journal of Artificial Intelligence in Education*, 20 (3), 197–229.

Duckworth, K., Akerman, R., MacGregor, A., Salter, E. and Vorhaus, J. (2009) *Self-regulated Learning: a literature review*. London: Centre for Research on the Wider Benefits of Learning, Institute of Education.

Duncan, T.G. and McKeachie, W.J. (2005) 'The making of the Motivated Strategies for Learning Questionnaire'. *Educational Psychologist*, 40 (2), 117–28.

Dweck, C.S. (1986) 'Motivational processes affecting learning'. *American Psychologist*, 41 (10), 1040–8.

Dweck, C.S. (2006). *Mindset: The new psychology of success*. New York: Random House.

Dweck, C.S. (2007) 'The perils and promises of praise'. *Educational Leadership*, 65 (2), 34–9.

Dweck, C.S. and Leggett, E.L. (1988) 'A social-cognitive approach to motivation and personality'. *Psychological Review*, 95 (2), 256–73.

Earle, S. (2017) 'Trolls, bots and fake news: The mysterious world of social media and manipulation'. *Newsweek,* 14 October. Online. www.newsweek.com/trolls-bots-and-fake-news-dark-and-mysterious-world-social-media-manipulation-682155 (accessed 11 February 2018).

EdPsychLab (n.d.) 'nStudy: A very brief overview'. Simon Fraser University. Online. www.sfu.ca/edpsychlab/nstudy.html (accessed 10 May 2018).

El-Hindi, A.E. (1996) 'Enhancing metacognitive awareness of college learners'. *Reading Horizons*, 36 (3), 214–30.

Elby, A. and Hammer, D. (2001) 'On the substance of a sophisticated epistemology'. *Science Education*, 85 (5), 554–67.

Elkin, J. (2014) 'Babies need books in the critical early years of life'. *New Review of Children's Literature and Librarianship*, 20 (1), 40–63.

Elliott, E.S. and Dweck, C.S. (1988) 'Goals: An approach to motivation and achievement'. *Journal of Personality and Social Psychology*, 54 (1), 5–12.

Elshout-Mohr, M., Meijer, J., van Daalen-Kapteijns, M.M. and Meeus, W. (2003) 'A self-report inventory for metacognition related to academic tasks'. Paper presented at the 10th biennial conference of the European Association for Research in Learning and Instruction, held in Padova, 26–30 August.

Ferrucci, D.A. (2012) 'Introduction to "This is Watson"'. *IBM Journal of Research and Development*, 56 (3.4) 1:1–1:15.

Fisher, M., Goddu, M., and Keil, F. (2015) 'Searching for explanations: How the internet inflates estimates of internal knowledge'. *Journal of Experimental Psychology*, 144 (3), 674–87. Online. www.apa.org/pubs/journals/releases/xge-0000070.pdf (accessed 9 May 2018).

Flavell, J.H. (1979) 'Metacognition and cognitive monitoring: A new area of cognitive-developmental inquiry'. *American Psychologist*, 34 (10), 906–11.

Frieman, S.M. (2014) 'Exam wrappers'. *Stanford Teaching Talk* blog, 1 June. Online. https://teachingcommons.stanford.edu/teaching-talk/exam-wrappers (accessed 9 May 2018).

Galton, M., Hargreaves, L., Comber, C., Wall, D. and Pell, T. (1999) 'Changes in patterns of teacher interaction in primary classrooms: 1976–96'. *British Educational Research Journal*, 25 (1), 23–37.

Gardner, H. (1983) *Frames of Mind: The theory of multiple intelligences*. New York: Basic Books.

Gattegno, C. (1974) *The Common Sense of Teaching Mathematics*. New York: Educational Solutions.

Gaved, M., Peasgood, A. and Kulkulska-Hulme, A. (2018) 'Learning when out and about'. In Luckin, R. (ed.) *Enhancing Learning with Technology: What the research says*. London: UCL IOE Press, 76–80.

Goleman, D.P. (1995) *Emotional Intelligence: Why it can matter more than IQ for character, health and lifelong achievement*. New York: Bantam Books.

Goodwin, C. (2007) 'Participation, stance, and affect in the organization of activities'. *Discourse and Society*, 18 (1), 53–73.

Goodwin, C. (2009) 'Calibrating bodies and cognition through interactive practice in a meaningful environment'. Keynote paper presented at a conference on Computer Supported Collaborative Learning, Rhodes, Greece, 8–13 June 2009.

Google (n.d.) 'Cloud AutoML'. Online. https://cloud.google.com/automl/ (accessed 4 April 2018).

Goos, M., Galbraith, P. and Renshaw, P. (2002) 'Socially mediated metacognition: Creating collaborative zones of proximal development in small group problem solving'. *Educational Studies in Mathematics*, 49 (2), 193–223.

Gottfredson, L.S. and Deary, I.J. (2016) 'Intelligence predicts health and longevity, but why?'. *Current Directions in Psychological Science*, 13 (1), 1–4. Online. http://journals.sagepub.com/doi/pdf/10.1111/j.0963-7214.2004.01301001.x (accessed 30 April 2018).

Graesser, A.C., D'Mello, S.K., Craig, S.D., Witherspoon, A., Sullins, J., McDaniel, B., and Gholson, B. (2008) 'The relationship between affective states and dialog patterns during interactions with AutoTutor'. *Journal of Interactive Learning Research*, 19 (2), 293–312.

Grist, M. (2009) 'Skills versus knowledge in education: A false dilemma'. RSA. Online www.thersa.org/discover/publications-and-articles/rsa-blogs/2009/05/skills-versus-knowledge-in-education-a-false-dilemma (accessed 4 April 2018).

Gunning, D. (n.d.) 'Explainable artificial intelligence (XAI)'. Defense Advanced Research Projects Agency. Online. www.darpa.mil/program/explainable-artificial-intelligence (accessed 4 April 2018).

Hammer, D. and Elby, A. (2002). 'On the form of a personal epistemology'. In Hofer, B.K. and Pintrich, P.R. (eds) *Personal Epistemology: The psychology of beliefs about knowledge and knowing*. Mahwah, NJ: Erlbaum, 169–90.

Hammer, D., Elby, A., Scherr, R.E. and Redish, E.F. (2005) 'Resources, framing, and transfer'. In Mestre, J. (ed.) *Transfer of Learning from a Modern Multidisciplinary Perspective*. Greenwich, CT: Information Age Publishing.

References

Hannon, V., Gillinson, S. and Shanks, L. with photographs by Reza (2013) *Learning a Living: Radical innovation in education for work*. London and New York: Bloomsbury.

Harackiewicz, J.M., Barron, K.E. and Elliot, A.J. (1998) 'Rethinking achievement goals: When are they adaptive for college students and why?' *Educational Psychologist*, 33 (1), 1–21.

Harris, A., Yuill, N. and Luckin, R. (2008) 'The influence of context-specific and dispositional achievement goals on children's paired collaborative interaction'. *British Journal of Educational Psychology*, 78 (3), 355–74.

Hattie, J., Biggs, J. and Purdie, N. (1996) 'Effects of learning skills interventions on student learning: A meta-analysis'. *Review of Educational Research*, 66, 99–126.

Haugeland, J. (1985) *Artificial Intelligence: The very idea*. Cambridge, MA and London: MIT Press.

Hern, A. (2017) 'Facebook and Twitter are being used to manipulate public opinion – report'. *The Guardian*, 19 June. Online. www.theguardian.com/technology/2017/jun/19/social-media-proganda-manipulating-public-opinion-bots-accounts-facebook-twitter (accessed 30 April 2018).

Higgins, S., Hall, E., Baumfield, V. and Moseley, D. (2005) *A Meta-analysis of the Impact of the Implementation of Thinking Skills Approaches on Pupils*. Research Evidence in Education Library. London: EPPI-Centre, Social Science Research Unit, Institute of Education.

Hinton, G.E. and Salakhutdinov, R.R. (2006) 'Reducing the dimensionality of data with neural networks'. *Science*, 313 (5786): 504–7.

Hinton, G., Li, D., Yu, D., Dahl, G., Mohamed, A.R., Jaitly, N., Senior, A., Vanhoucke, V., Nguyen, P., Sainath, T. and Kingsbury, B. (2012) 'Deep neural networks for acoustic modeling in speech recognition'. Signal Processing Magazine, 29 (6), 82–97.

Hofer, B. and Pintrich, P. (1997) 'The development of epistemological theories: Beliefs about knowledge and knowing and their relation to learning'. *Review of Educational Research*, 67 (1), 88–140.

Hofer, R. and Pintrich, P. (2002) *Personal Epistemology: The psychology of beliefs about knowledge and knowing*. Mahwah, NJ: Lawrence Erlbaum Associates.

House of Lords Artificial Intelligence Committee (2017). 'AI in the UK: Ready, willing and able?' Report of session 2017–19, published 16 April 2017. HL Paper 100. Online. https://publications.parliament.uk/pa/ld201719/ldselect/ldai/100/10002.htm (accessed 9 May 2018).

Husbands, C. and Pearce, J. (2012) 'What is great pedagogy: A literature review for the National College of School Leadership'. National College for School Leadership. Online. www.redhilltsa.org.uk/pluginfile.php/376/mod_resource/content/0/research-and-development-network-lit-review-theme-one.pdf (accessed 30 April 2018).

Hutchins, E. (1995) *Cognition in the Wild*. Cambridge, MA: MIT Press.

Hutson, M. (2017) 'How Google is making music with artificial intelligence'. *Science*, 8 August. Online. www.sciencemag.org/news/2017/08/how-google-making-music-artificial-intelligence (accessed 5 April 2018).

Jackson, A.W. and Davis, G.A. (2000) *Turning Points 2000: Educating adolescents in the 21st century*. New York: Teachers College Press.

Jackson, D.N. (2002) 'Evaluating g in the SAT: Implications for the sex differences and interpretations of verbal and quantitative aptitude'. Paper presented at the International Society for Intelligence Research, Nashville, Tennessee, 5–7 December.

Järvenoja, H. and Järvelä, S. (2013) 'Regulating emotions together for motivated collaboration'. In Baker, M., Andriessen, J. and Järvelä, S. (eds) *Affective Learning Together: Social and emotional dimensions of collaborative learning*. London and New York: Routledge, 162–81.

Johnes, R. (2017) 'Entries to arts subjects at Key Stage 4'. London: Education Policy Institute. Online. https://epi.org.uk/wp-content/uploads/2018/01/EPI-Entries-to-arts-KS4-1.pdf (accessed 5 April 2018).

Johnson, L.W. (2007) 'Serious use of a serious game for language learning'. In Luckin, R., Koedinger, K.R. and Greer, J. (eds) *Proceedings of the 2007 Conference on Artificial Intelligence in Education: Building technology rich learning contexts that work* (Frontiers in Artificial Intelligence and Applications 158). Amsterdam: IOS Press, 67–74.

Johnson, S. (1998) *Who Moved My Cheese? An amazing way to deal with change in your work and in your life*. New York: Putnam.

Kahneman, D. (2011) *Thinking, Fast and Slow*. New York: Farrar, Strauss, Giroux.

Kahneman, D. and Tversky, A. (eds) (2000) *Choices, Values and Frames*. New York: Cambridge University Press.

Kapoor, A., Burleson, W. and Picard, R. (2007) 'Automatic prediction of frustration'. *International Journal of Human-Computer Studies*, 65 (8), 724–36.

Kim, Y. (2007) 'Desirable characteristics of learning companions'. *International Journal of Artificial Intelligence in Education*, 17 (4), 371–88.

King, P.M. and Kitchener, K.S. (1994) *Developing Reflective Judgment: Understanding and promoting intellectual growth and critical thinking in adolescents and adults*. San Francisco: Jossey-Bass.

King, P.M. and Kitchener, K.S. (2002) 'The reflective judgment model: Twenty years of research on epistemic cognition'. In Hofer, B. and Pintrich, P.R. (eds) *Personal Epistemology: The psychology of beliefs about knowledge and knowing*. Mahwah, NJ: Lawrence Erlbaum Associates, 37–61.

King, P.M. and Kitchener, K.S. (2004) 'Reflective judgement: Theory and research on the development of epistemic assumptions through adulthood'. *Educational Psychologist*, 39 (1), 5–18.

Klassen, R.M., Bong, M., Usher, E.L., Chong, W.H., Huan, V.S., Wong, I.Y. and Georgiou, T. (2009) 'Exploring the validity of a teachers' self-efficacy scale in five countries'. *Contemporary Educational Psychology*, 34 (1), 67–76.

Kleinsmith, A., De Silva, P.R. and Bianchi-Berhouze, N. (2005) 'Recognizing emotion from postures: Cross-cultural differences in user modelling'. In Ardissono, L., Brna, P. and Mitrovic, A. (eds) *User Modeling 2005: 10th international conference, UM 2005, Edinburgh, Scotland, UK, July 24–29, 2005: proceedings*. Lecture Notes in Artificial Intelligence 3538. Berlin and New York: Springer, 50–59.

Koedinger, K.R., Corbett, A.C. and Perfetti, C. (2012) 'The knowledge-learning-instruction (KLI) framework: Bridging the science-practice chasm to enhance robust student learning'. *Cognitive Science*, 36 (5), 757–98.

References

Kornell, N. (2009) 'Metacognition in humans and animals'. *Current Directions in Psychological Science*, 18 (1), 11–15.

Kuang, C. (2017) 'Can AI be taught to explain itself?' *The New York Times Magazine*, 21 November. Online. www.nytimes.com/2017/11/21/magazine/can-ai-be-taught-to-explain-itself.html (accessed 4 April 2018).

Kuhn, D. (2001) 'How do people know?' *Psychological Science,* 12 (1), 1–8.

Kuhn, D. and Weinstock, M. (2002) 'What is epistemological thinking and why does it matter?' In Hofer, B. and Pintrich, P.R. (eds) *Personal Epistemology: The psychology of beliefs about knowledge and knowing.* Mahwah, NJ: Lawrence Erlbaum Associates, 121–44.

Kuhn, T.S. (1962) *The Structure of Scientific Revolutions.* Chicago: University of Chicago Press.

Kutnick, P. and Blatchford, P. (2013) *Effective Group-work in Primary School Classrooms: The SPRinG approach.* Dordrecht: Springer.

Kutnick, P., Blatchford, P. and Baines, E. (2002) 'Pupil groupings in primary school classrooms: Sites for learning and social pedagogy?' *British Educational Research Journal*, 28 (2), 188–206.

Kutnick, P., Blatchford, P. and Baines, E. (2005). 'Grouping of pupils in secondary school classrooms: Possible links between pedagogy and learning'. *Social Psychology of Education*, 8, 349e374.

Lakatos, I., Worrall, J. and Zahar, E. (1976) *Proofs and Refutations: The logic of mathematical discovery.* Cambridge: Cambridge University Press.

Lave, J. and Wenger, E. (1991) *Situated Learning: Legitimate peripheral participation.* Cambridge: Cambridge University Press.

Lazarus, R. (1991) 'Cognition and motivation in education'. *American Psychologist*, 46 (4), 352–67.

Lee, J. (2009) 'Universals and specifics of math self-concept, math self-efficacy, and math anxiety across 41 PISA 2003 participating countries'. *Learning and Individual Differences*, 19 (3), 355–65.

Leelawong, K. and Biswas, G. (2008) 'Designing learning by teaching agents: The Betty's Brain system'. *International Journal of Artificial Intelligence in Education*, 18 (3), 181–208.

Lewis, J. and Cowie, H. (1993) 'Cooperative group work: promises and limitations. A study of teachers' values'. *BPS Education Section Review*, 17 (2), 77–84.

Lewis, M. (2011) *The Big Short.* London: Penguin.

Lindqvist, M. (2015) 'Gaining and sustaining TEL in a 1:1 laptop initiative: Possibilities and challenges for teachers and students'. *Computers In The Schools*, 32 (1), 35–62. DOI: 10.1080/07380569.2015.1004274.

Lucas, B., Claxton, G. and Spencer, E. (2013) *Progression in Student Creativity in School: First steps towards new forms of formative assessments.* OECD Education Working Papers No. 86. Paris: OECD Publishing.

Luckin, R. (2010) *Re-designing Learning Contexts: Technology-rich, learner-centred ecologies.* London: Routledge.

Luckin, R. (2017a) 'Towards artificial intelligence-based assessment systems'. *Nature Human Behaviour*, 1, article number 0028. DOI: 10.1038/s41562-016-0028.

Luckin, R. (2017b) 'The implications of artificial intelligence for teachers and schooling'. In Loble, L., Creenaline, T. and Hayes, J. (eds) *Future Frontiers: Education for an AI world*. Carlton, Victoria: Melbourne University Press and New South Wales Department of Education, 109–26.

Luckin, R. (n.d.) 'The knowledge illusion'. Online. https://knowledgeillusion.blog (accessed 10 February 2018).

Luckin, R. and du Boulay, B. (2001) 'Embedding AIED in ie-TV through Broadband User Modelling (BbUM)'. In Moore, J., Johnson, W.L. and Redfield, C.L. (eds) *Artificial Intelligence in Education: AI-ED in the Wired and Wireless Future*. Proceedings of the 10th International Conference on Artificial Intelligence in Education, held in San Antonio, TX, 19–23 May 2001. Amsterdam: IOS Press, 322–33.

Luckin, R. and du Boulay, B. (2017) 'Reflections on the Ecolab and the zone of proximal development'. *International Journal of Artificial Intelligence in Education*, 26 (1), 416–30. DOI: 10.1007/s40593-015-0072-x

Luckin, R., Baines, E., Cukurova, M. and Holmes, W. with Mann, M. (2017) *Solved! Making the case for collaborative problem-solving*. London: Nesta. Online. www.nesta.org.uk/sites/default/files/solved-making-case-collaborative-problem-solving.pdf (accessed 15 February 2018).

Luckin, R., Holmes, W., Forcier, L. and Griffiths, M. (2016) *Intelligence Unleashed: An argument for AI in education*. London: Pearson Education. Online. www.pearson.com/content/dam/one-dot-com/one-dot-com/global/Files/about-pearson/innovation/Intelligence-Unleashed-Publication.pdf (accessed 30 April 2018).

Luckin, R., Bligh, B., Manches, A., Ainsworth, S., Crook, C. and Noss, R. (2012) *Decoding Learning: The proof, promise and potential of educational technology*. London: Nesta. Online. www.nesta.org.uk/sites/default/files/decoding_learning_report.pdf (accessed 30 April 2018).

Maldonado, H., Lee, B., Klemmer, S.R. and Pea, R. (2007) 'Patterns of collaboration in design courses: Team dynamics affect technology appropriation, artifact creation, and course performance'. Paper presented at the eighth International Conference on Computer-supported Collaborative Learning, held in New Brunswick, NJ, 16–21 July 2007.

Manovich, L. (2006) 'The poetics of augmented space'. *Visual Communication*, 5 (2), 219–40.

Marzano, R. (1998) 'A theory-based meta-analysis of research on instruction'. Online. www.faculty.mun.ca/cmattatall/WhatWorks-Marzano.pdf (accessed 2 May 2017).

McCambridge, R. (2014) 'Legacy of a failed foundation initiative: inBloom, Gates and Carnegie'. *Nonprofit Quarterly*. Online. https://nonprofitquarterly.org/policysocial-context/24452-legacy-of-a-failed-foundation-initiative- inbloom-gates-and-carnegie.html (accessed 30 April 2018).

McCulloch, W.S. and Pitts, W. (1943) 'A logical calculus of the ideas immanent in nervous activity'. *Bulletin of Mathematical Biophysics*, 5 (4), 115–33.

References

McQuiggan, S.W. and Lester, J.C. (2006) 'Diagnosing self-efficacy in intelligent tutoring systems: An empirical study'. In Ikeda, M., Ashley, K.D. and Chan, T.-W. (eds) *Intelligent Tutoring Systems*. Proceedings of the eighth international Intelligent Tutoring Systems conference, held in Jhongli, Taiwan, 26–30 June 2006. Lecture Notes in Computer Science, 4053. Berlin and New York: Springer, 565–73.

Mitchnick, D., Clemens, C., Kagereki, J., Kumar, V., Kinshuk and Fraser, S. (2017) 'Measuring the written language disorder among students with Attention Deficit Hyperactivity Disorder'. *Journal of Writing Analytics*, 1, 147–75.

MIT Technology Review (2015) 'Deep learning machine beats humans in IQ test'. Online. www.technologyreview.com/s/538431/deep-learning-machine-beats-humans-in-iq-test/ (accessed 4 April 2018).

Mohamad, Y., Velasco, C.A., Damm, S. and Tebarth, H. (2004) 'Cognitive training with animated pedagogical agents (TAPA) in children with learning disabilities'. In Miesenberger, K., Klaus, J., Zagler, W.L. and Burger, D. (eds) *Computers Helping People with Special Needs*. Proceedings of the ninth ICCHP International Conference, held in Paris, 7–9 July. Berlin: Springer, 187–93. Online. https://link.springer.com/chapter/10.1007/978-3-540-27817-7_28 (accessed 9 May 2018).

New York Times (n.d.) 'Harvard exams, 1899'. Online. http://graphics8.nytimes.com/packages/pdf/education/harvardexam.pdf (accessed 4 April 2018).

OECD (2017) *PISA 2015 Results (Volume 5): Collaborative problem solving*. Paris: OECD Publishing. Online. www.oecd-ilibrary.org/docserver/download/9817051e.pdf?expires=1518697877&id=id&accname=guest&checksum=20C57780420DF0BDB1D6C1AC324374F0 (accessed 15 February 2018).

OECD (2018) 'Programme for International Student Assessment'. Online. www.oecd.org/pisa/ (accessed 4 April 2018).

OECD TALIS (2013) 'The OECD Teaching and Learning International Survey (TALIS) – 2013 results'. Online. www.oecd.org/education/school/talis-2013-results.htm (accessed 9 May 2018).

O'Neil, H.F. and Abedi, J. (1996) 'Reliability and validity of a state metacognitive inventory: Potential for alternative assessment'. *Journal of Educational Research*, 89 (4), 234–45.

Ortony, A., Clore, G.L. and Collins, A. (1988) *The Cognitive Structure of Emotions*. Cambridge: Cambridge University Press.

Owen, D. and Vista, A. (2017) 'Strategies for teaching metacognition in classrooms'. *Brookings*. Online. www.brookings.edu/blog/education-plus-development/2017/11/15/strategies-for-teaching-metacognition-in-classrooms/ (accessed 4 April 2018).

Palincsar, A.S. and Brown, A.L. (1984) 'Reciprocal teaching of comprehension-fostering and comprehension-monitoring activities'. *Cognition and Instruction*, 1 (2), 117–75.

Pekrun, R., Goetz, T., Titz, W. and Perry, R. (2002) 'Academic emotions in students' learning and achievement: A program of qualitative and quantitative research'. *Educational Psychologist*, 37 (2), 91–105.

Performance Learning (n.d.) 'Performance Learning'. Online. http://myperformancelearning.com/ (accessed 4 April 2018).

Picard, R.W. (2000) *Affective Computing*. Cambridge, MA: MIT Press.

Pintrich, P.R. (2000a) 'An achievement goal theory perspective on issues in motivation terminology, theory, and research'. *Contemporary Educational Psychology*, 25 (1), 92–104.

Pintrich, P.R. (2000b) 'The role of goal orientation in self-regulated learning'. In Boekarts, J. Pintrich, P. and Zeidner, M. (eds) *Handbook of Self-Regulation*. Burlington, MA: Elsevier Academic Press, 451–502.

Pintrich, P., Smith, D., Garcia, T. and McKeachie, W. (1993) 'Reliability and predictive validity of the Motivated Strategies for Learning Questionnaire (MSLQ)'. In *Educational and Psychological Measurement*, 53 (3), 801–13.

Popper, K. (1982) *Unended Quest: An Intellectual Autobiography*. La Salle, IL: Open Court.

QCA (2004) *Creativity: Find it, promote it*. London: QCA Publications.

Quora (2016) 'Albert Einstein reportedly said: "The true sign of intelligence is not knowledge, but imagination". What did he mean?' Online. www.quora.com/Albert-Einstein-reportedly-said-The-true-sign-of-intelligence-is-not-knowledge-but-imagination-What-did-he-mean (accessed 4 April 2018).

Rajendran, T., Porayska-Pomsta, K., Smith, T., Lemon, O. and the ECHOES consortium (2013) 'The ECHOES technology enhanced environment: Facilitating social communication skills in children with autism'. Poster presented at the International Meeting for Autism Research held in San Sebastian, 3 May.

Reading Rockets (2014) 'Students take charge: Reciprocal teaching'. Online video. www.youtube.com/watch?v=My68SDGeTHI (accessed 9 May 2018).

Roach, J. (2018) 'Microsoft researchers build a bot that draws what you tell it to'. *The AI Blog*. Microsoft, 18 January. Online. https://blogs.microsoft.com/ai/drawing-ai/ (accessed 5 April 2018).

Rogoff, B., Malkin, C. and Gilbride, K. (1984) 'Interaction with babies as guidance in development'. *New Directions for Child Development*, 23, 31–44.

Rosenblatt, F. (1957) 'The Perceptron – a perceiving and recognizing automaton'. Report 85-460-1, Cornell Aeronautical Laboratory.

Rosenshine, B. (2012) 'Principles of instruction: Research-based strategies that all teachers should know'. *American Educator*, Spring 2012, 12–39. Online. www.aft.org/pdfs/americaneducator/spring2012/Rosenshine.pdf (accessed 30 April 2018).

Roth, B., Becker, N., Romeyke, S., Schäfer, S., Domnick, F. and Spinath, F.M. (2015) 'Intelligence and school grades: A meta-analysis'. *Intelligence*, 53, 118–37.

Ryan, R.M. and Deci, E.L. (2000) 'Intrinsic and extrinsic motivations: Classic definitions and new directions'. *Contemporary Educational Psychology*, 25, 54–67.

Ryan, R.M. and Deci, E.L. (2002) 'An overview of self-determination theory: An organismic-dialectical perspective'. In Deci, E.L. and Ryan, R.M. (eds) *Handbook of Self-determination Research*. Rochester, NY: University of Rochester Press, 3–33.

Salovey, P. and Mayer, J.D. (1990) 'Emotional intelligence'. *Imagination, Cognition, and Personality*, 9, 185–211.

Sandoval, W.A. (2003) 'Conceptual and epistemic aspects of students' scientific explanations'. *Journal of the Learning Sciences*, 12 (1), 5–52.

Schommer-Aikins, M. (2004) 'Explaining the epistemological belief system: Introducing the embedded systemic model and coordinated research approach'. *Educational Psychologist*, 39 (1), 19–29.

Schraw, G. (1998) 'Promoting general metacognitive awareness'. *Instructional Science*, 26 (1–2), 113–25.

Scott, S. (2008) 'Perceptions of students' learning critical thinking through debate in a technology classroom: A case study'. *The Journal of Technology Studies*, 34 (1), 39–44.

SEAL Community (n.d.) 'About SEAL'. Online. www.sealcommunity.org/node/356 (accessed 9 April 2018).

Sefton-Green, J., Thomson, P., Jones, K. and Bresler, L. (eds) (2011) *The Routledge International Handbook of Creative Learning*. London: Routledge.

Shabani, K. (2016) 'Applications of Vygotsky's sociocultural approach for teachers' professional development'. *Cogent Education*, 3 (1). DOI: 10.1080/2331186X.2016.1252177.

Simon, H.A. (1996) *The Sciences of the Artificial*. 3rd ed. Cambridge, MA: MIT Press.

Skaalvik, E.M. and Skaalvik, S. (2007) 'Dimensions of teacher self-efficacy and relations with strain factors, perceived collective teacher efficacy, and teacher burnout'. *Journal of Educational Psychology*, 99 (3), 611–25.

Skinner, B.F. (1957) *Verbal Behavior*. Acton, MA: Copley Publishing Group.

Skinner, B.F. (1991) *The Behavior of Organisms: An experimental analysis*. Acton, MA: Copley Publishing Group.

Smith, J.R. (2016) 'IBM research takes Watson to Hollywood with the first "cognitive movie trailer"'. *THINK Blog*, IBM, 31 August. Online. www.ibm.com/blogs/think/2016/08/cognitive-movie-trailer/ (accessed 5 April 2018).

Soller, A. and Lesgold, A. (2003) 'A computational approach to analyzing online knowledge sharing interaction'. In Hoppe, U., Verdejo, F. and Kay, J. (eds) *Artificial Intelligence in Education: Shaping the future of learning through intelligent technologies*. Frontiers in Artificial Intelligence and Applications, 97. Amsterdam: IOS Press, 253–68.

Sorrel, J., Roberts, P. and Henley, D. (2014) *The Virtuous Circle: Why creativity and cultural education count*. London: Elliot & Thompson Ltd.

Spearman, C. (2005) *The Abilities of Man: Their nature and measurement*. Originally 1927. Caldwell, NJ: The Blackburn Press.

Stanovich, K. and West, R. (2008) 'On the relative independence of thinking biases and cognitive ability'. *Journal of Personality and Social Psychology*, 94 (4), 672–95.

Stanovich, K.E. (2009a) *What Intelligence Tests Miss: The psychology of rational thought*. 1st ed. New Haven, CT: Yale University Press.

Stanovich, K.E. (2009b) *Decision Making and Rationality in the Modern World*. New York: Oxford University Press.

Stanovich, K.E. (2016) *The Rationality Quotient: Toward a test of rational thinking*. 1st ed. Cambridge, MA: MIT Press.

Stelar – STEM Learning and Research Center (n.d.) 'Motivated strategies for learning questionnaire (MSLQ)'. Online. http://stelar.edc.org/instruments/motivated-strategies-learning-questionnaire-mslq (accessed 9 May 2018).

Sternberg, R.J. (1985) *Beyond IQ: A triarchic theory of human intelligence.* Cambridge: Cambridge University Press.

Sternberg, R.J. (1999) *The Handbook of Creativity.* Cambridge and New York: Cambridge University Press.

Sweller, J. and Sweller, S. (2006) 'Natural information processing systems'. *Evolutionary Psychology,* 4 (1), 434–58. DOI: 10.1177/147470490600400135.

Sylva, K., Melhuish, E., Sammons, P., Siraj-Blatchford, I. and Taggart, B. (eds) (2010) *Early Childhood Matters: Evidence from the Effective Preschool and Primary Education Project.* London: Routledge.

Tarricone, P. (2011) *The Taxonomy of Metacognition.* New York: Psychology Press.

Tegmark, M. (2017) *Life 3.0: Being Human in the Age of Artificial Intelligence.* London: Allen Lane.

Thaler, R.H. and Sunstein, C.R. (2008) *Nudge: Improving decisions about health, wealth, and happiness.* New Haven, CT: Yale University Press.

The Economist (2017) 'The world's most valuable resource is no longer oil, but data'. *The Economist.* Online. www.economist.com/news/leaders/21721656-data-economy-demands-new-approach-antitrust-rules-worlds-most-valuable-resource (accessed 13 February 2018).

Thorndike, E.L. (1911) *Individuality.* Boston: Houghton Mifflin.

Thorndike, E.L. (1914) *Educational Psychology.* New York: Teachers College, Columbia University.

Titcomb, J. and Carson, J. (2018) 'Fake news: What exactly is it – and how can you spot it?' *The Telegraph,* 29 January. Online. www.telegraph.co.uk/technology/0/fake-news-exactly-has-really-had-influence/ (accessed 11 February 2018).

Trilling, B. and Fadel, C. (2009) *21st Century Skills: Learning for life in our times.* San Francisco: Jossey-Bass.

Turing, A. (1950) 'Computing machinery and intelligence'. *Mind,* 49, 433–60.

Valsiner, J. (1984) 'Construction of the zone of proximal development in adult-child joint action: The socialisation of meals'. In Rogoff, B. and Wertsch, J.V. (eds) *Children's Learning in the 'Zone of Proximal Development'.* San Francisco: Jossey-Bass, 65–76.

Vanderbilt University (2014) 'Betty's Brain'. The Teachable Agents Group at Vanderbilt University. Online. www.teachableagents.org/research/bettysbrain.php (accessed 4 April 2018).

Vizcaíno, A. (2005) 'A simulated student can improve collaborative learning'. *International Journal of Artificial Intelligence in Education,* 15 (1), 3–40.

Vygotsky, L.S. (1978) *Mind in Society: The development of higher psychological processes.* Trans. Cole, M., John-Steiner, V., Scribner, S. and Souberman, E. Cambridge, MA: Harvard University Press.

Vygotsky, L.S. (1986) *Thought and Language.* Cambridge, MA: MIT Press.

Vygotsky, L.S. (1987) *The Collected Works of L.S. Vygotsky.* Vol. 1. New York: Plenum.

Watson, J.B. (1926) 'Experimental studies on the growth of the emotions'. In Murchison, C. (ed.) *Psychologies of 1925.* Worcester, MA: Clark University Press.

References

Webb, N. and Palincsar, A.S. (1996) 'Group processes in the classroom'. In Berliner, D.C. and Calfee, R.C. (eds) *Handbook of Educational Psychology*. New York: Macmillan, 841–73.

Wheelahan, L. (2015) 'Not just skills: What a focus on knowledge means for vocational education'. *Journal of Curriculum Studies*, 47 (6), 750–62.

Whitney, L. (2017) 'Are computers already smarter than humans?' *TIME*. Online. http://time.com/4960778/computers-smarter-than-humans/ (accessed 4 April 2018).

Wiener, N. (1950) *The Human Use of Human Beings: Cybernetics and society*. Boston: Houghton Mifflin.

Wikipedia (n.d.a.) 'AlphaGo versus Lee Sedol'. Online. https://en.wikipedia.org/wiki/AlphaGo_versus_Lee_Sedol (accessed 9 February 2018).

Wikipedia (n.d.b.) 'I know that I know nothing'. Online. https://en.wikipedia.org/wiki/I_know_that_I_know_nothing (accessed 4 April 2018).

Wikipedia (n.d.c.) 'R.U.R.' Online. https://en.wikipedia.org/wiki/R.U.R. (accessed 4 April 2018).

Wikipedia (n.d.d.) 'Internet of things'. Online. https://en.wikipedia.org/wiki/Internet_of_things (accessed 10 May 2018).

Wiliam, D. (2012) 'Metacognition – Dylan Wiliam – Learning and teaching'. Online. Video. www.youtube.com/watch?v=bojaoVYrBmE (accessed 9 May 2018).

W.K. Kellogg Foundation (2006) 'Logic model development guide'. Online. www.wkkf.org/resource-directory/resource/2006/02/wk-kellogg-foundation-logic-model-development-guide (accessed 30 April 2018).

Wolfe, M. and Williams, T.J. (2017) 'Poor metacognitive awareness of belief change'. *Quarterly Journal of Experimental Psychology*, 12, 1–45. DOI: 10.1080/17470218.2017.1363792.

Wolters, C.A. and Daugherty, S.G. (2007) 'Goal structures and teachers' sense of efficacy: Their relation and association to teaching experience and academic level'. *Journal of Educational Psychology*, 99, 181–93.

Wood, D. (1990) *How Children Think and Learn: The social contexts of cognitive development*. Oxford: Basil Blackwell.

Wood, K. (1997) *Interdisciplinary Instruction: A practical guide for elementary and middle school teachers*. Upper Saddle River, NJ: Merrill.

Woolfolk Hoy, A. and Burke Spero, R. (2005) 'Changes in teacher efficacy during the early years of teaching: A comparison of four measures'. *Teaching and Teacher Education*, 21 (4), 343–56.

World Economic Forum (2015) *New Visions of Education: Unlocking the potential of technology*. Geneva: World Economic Forum. Online. www3.weforum.org/docs/WEFUSA_NewVisionforEducation_Report2015.pdf (accessed 15 February 2018).

Yasnitsky, A. and van der Veer, R. (eds) (2015) *Revisionist Revolution in Vygotsky Studies: The state of the art*. London and New York: Routledge.

Index

Index